Jean-Georges Vongerichten

SIMPLE CUISINE

Macmillan • USA

MACMILLAN
A Simon & Schuster Macmillan Company
1633 Broadway
New York, NY 10019-6785

Macmillan Publishing books may be purchased for
business or sales promotion use. For information please
write: Special Markets Department, Macmillan Publishing
USA, 1633 Broadway, New York, NY 10019.

MACMILLAN is a registered trademark of Macmillan, Inc.

Library of Congress Cataloging-in-Publication Data
  Vongerichten, Jean-Georges.
  Simple Cuisine/Jean-Georges Vongerichten
   p. cm.
  ISBN 0-02-860991-3
  1. Cookery, French. I. Title
  TX719.V66 1990
  641.5944-dc20   89-78154
        CIP

Book design by Amy Trombat

Manufactured in the United States of America
10 9 8 7 6 5 4 3 2 1

SIMPLE CUISINE

Acknowledgments

I want to thank a few of the people who helped me bring forth my first book. Many thanks to all the cooks in my kitchen who assisted me these past four years in developing the new styles and concepts I now bring you.

To Lois Freedman, one of my cooks, special thanks for helping me translate and unravel the mysteries of ingredients and preparation into the simplicity of these recipes.

To my friend Michael Futterman, many thanks for his advice, help, and constant encouragement during the year-and-a-half adventure of writing *Simple Cuisine*.

Contents

Introduction

A New Approach to Fast Cooking

Asked by many friends, magazines, and newspapers for my recipes over the last few years, I realized finally that my new style of cooking is ideal for the home cook. It is the very answer for anyone who wants to prepare memorable meals but feels put off by complicated recipes. To these home cooks, I heartily dedicate this book.

By 1987, with Restaurant Lafayette open one year and a three-star award from *The New York Times*, I began experimenting with a new approach. I was looking for a way to give foods more intense flavor, as well as make them lighter, fresher. As it happened, the dishes I discovered along the way were also astonishingly rapid to prepare.

I dropped those elements of classic and nouvelle cooking that take considerable time and effort. My new cuisine relies on the simplicity of lightly steamed and sautéed foods, and limits the use of cream, butter, and flour. With a handful of simple sauces and broths (today I think of them as my "basics"), I realized a virtually limitless variety of fabulous combinations and, in the process, shaped a new approach to cooking.

This new approach maximizes ease of preparation, lightness, and visual appeal. Here is how it works: To replace traditional basics of French cooking (such as time-consuming stocks and butter-thick sauces), I use "building blocks." They are:

Juices   Vinaigrettes   Flavored Oils   Broths

A fifth basic ingredient, phyllo dough, replaces puff pastry. With these building blocks, everything from appetizers and seafood to poultry and meats can be prepared with a thrillingly fresh point of view and—here's the best part—in very little time. Innovative seasonal fruit desserts, ice creams, sorbets, and granités were a natural extension of our new approach, and many are included in this book.

Our customers at the restaurant were very enthusiastic about the new and simple directions we were taking. It was always my hope to please not just those people who take food very seriously but the diner who samples our food on a birthday or other special occasion. We must have been doing something right, for in April 1988, *The New York Times* awarded us its highest rating: four stars.

Before preparing the dishes I offer in this book, make a few of the basics first—a vegetable juice, a flavored oil, a vinaigrette, a vegetable broth. Once you have prepared a few of the building blocks, you will know essentially all there is to know about how these basics can become a mainstay of your everyday cooking. You can come home at the end of the day with a nice piece of fish or steak and, ten minutes later, sit down to a marvelous meal. Turn to page 86, "Simple Sautés and Steamed Dishes," and see how easy it is to quickly sauté or steam fish, shellfish, poultry, or meat and combine it perfectly with the basics. With three or four flavored oils and vinaigrettes in the cupboard and refrigerator (and with the rapid preparation of juices and broths), you'll immediately feel freer to cook not only more creatively, but more quickly too.

In addition to chapters that highlight the building blocks, I've included a chapter on foie gras. It is probably the most luxurious food known to mankind—one I wouldn't want to live without—and simpler to prepare than you might think. Also included are chapters that reflect my love of Asian flavors, some rather special side dishes, my interpretation of some American classics (such as hamburgers, shrimp cocktail, and a tuna "sandwich"), and, of course, desserts.

Finally, I've included lots of menus. Use them for inspiration or to help with those times we all have occasionally, when we just run out of ideas. If you need a menu for a special occasion, or want to put together a wonderful meal in thirty minutes or less, look here.

Most of my recipes are uncomplicated. Some take a little more time than others, but I think you'll find the results speak for themselves. A word on presentation: It is something that has always been important to me, and you should feel free to experiment, just as you would with seasoning, to suit your own taste and please yourself.

It hasn't been easy to set out on a new path in cooking, particularly when the cuisine of my mentors and fellow chefs is so special. I hope that the ideas and small innovations you find in these pages inspire you as they have me, and that they become a comfortable and exciting part of your life in the kitchen.

Most important to me is that you let your imagination go—and have fun.

Amitiés Gourmandes,
Jean-Georges Vongerichten
New York City

building block
Juices

THE PRIMARY ELEMENT OF MY CUISINE IS THE USE OF VEGETABLE JUICES—AND THE OCCASIONAL FRUIT JUICE—SIMPLE, RICHLY FLAVORED SAUCES BY THEMSELVES AND IN COMBINATION WITH FLAVORED OILS. One morning, several years ago, I prepared myself a glass of carrot juice as a little "pick-me-up," and suddenly I realized that—with only a little seasoning—it would serve as a perfect complement to shellfish. I prepared it as a sauce and it was exquisite. This new preparation had the three characteristics a sauce needs to be great: body (texture), seasoning, and acidity. This carrot sauce, my first vegetable juice recipe, appears on pages 1 and 9.

The vegetable juices must be made with a vegetable juicer. Juicers I have used and recommend are the ACME Model 6001, the Waring Model PJE 40 or the Champion. All are available in kitchen supply stores featuring food processors and similar equipment. Remember: Vegetable juices can't be made with citrus juicers or standard food processors, because they don't separate juice from pulp.

The preparation of the juice sauces takes less than 5 minutes. The vegetables and fruits used in the recipes that follow are:

Carrots	Fennel
Zucchini	Asparagus
Celery	Broccoli
Leeks	Beets
Peppers (Yellow, Green, and Red)	Pineapples
	Oranges
Radishes	Grapefruit

Each recipe that calls for a vegetable juice will specify the amount of the vegetable needed to make the appropriate amount of juice. Preparation of a vegetable juice sauce begins by feeding the raw, scrubbed vegetable through the juicer as the manufacturer directs. Always use the recommended amount of juice. If more is needed, run another vegetable through the juicer. To the raw juice we add some seasoning and a touch of oil or a little butter. This mixture is cooked over low heat until it just boils. It's better to prepare the sauce just before it's needed.

note *Most vegetables contain a considerable amount of water, and the sauce may separate. Don't worry. Leave the sauce on very low heat for a few moments while whisking briskly. Whisk again just before serving.*

EXAMPLES

SPICY CARROT JUICE

MAKES 2 CUPS
(USE ½ CUP PER SERVING)

Peel 10 medium carrots.

Put the carrots through a juice extractor. You should have 2 cups of juice.

In a saucepan, combine the carrot juice and a pinch each of ground cinnamon, ground clove, ground nutmeg, salt, and cayenne pepper. Add 4 tablespoons cold sweet butter, cut into pieces.

Bring the mixture to a boil over medium-low heat, whisking constantly.

As soon as the sauce reaches a boil, take it off the heat. If not serving it immediately, keep it warm over low heat.

ZUCCHINI JUICE WITH THYME

MAKES 2 ¾ CUPS
(USE ½ CUP PER SERVING)

Put 4 large zucchini (unpeeled) through a juice extractor. You should have 2 cups of juice.

In a saucepan, combine the zucchini juice, ¾ cup extra virgin olive oil, and 2 tablespoons whole fresh thyme leaves or 2 teaspoons dried.

Bring the mixture to a boil over medium-low heat, whisking constantly.

As soon as the sauce reaches a boil, take it off the heat. If not serving it immediately, keep it warm over low heat.

In addition to their use in the recipes that follow, the vegetable juice sauces complement perfectly the quick sautés and steamed dishes of chicken, veal, fish, and shellfish on pages 86 to 94.

Smoked Salmon Custard
with Fennel Juice

Use a steamer when preparing any custard. When you bake a custard, even using a water bath (a bain marie), you will have a grainy custard with little holes. Steaming, a method that uses indirect heat, avoids this and gives you perfectly smooth results. If nonstick ramekins are not available, use ceramic ones lined with plastic wrap.

SERVES 4

41 cup diced smoked salmon (8 ounces)	5 medium bulbs fennel, coarsely chopped (leaves reserved for garnish)
1 cup milk	
2 eggs	2 tablespoons sweet butter plus additional butter for the molds
1 tablespoon plus $1/2$ teaspoon fresh lime juice	$1/4$ teaspoon fennel seeds
Salt and cayenne pepper to taste	

Put the salmon and milk in a food processor or blender. Process to a smooth purée.

Whisk together the purée, eggs, 1 tablespoon lime juice, salt, and cayenne pepper until well combined.

Put the fennel through a juice extractor. You should have 2 cups of juice. Add $1/2$ teaspoon lime juice.

Lightly butter four 2-ounce nonstick ramekins and fill them with the salmon mixture. Place the ramekins in a steamer and cover tightly. Steam for 7 minutes or until the custard is set. Unmold onto serving plates, using a sharp knife if necessary to help loosen the sides.

Heat the fennel juice mixture, butter, and fennel seeds just to boiling. Spoon a little of the sauce over the custard. Garnish with fennel leaves.

Yellow Pike with Celery Juice

Yellow pike is the natural cross of northern pike (brochet) and perch. Brochet has too many bones to enjoy as fillets, but it is superb in quenelles or a fish terrine. Yellow pike is a wonderful fish with the flavor of northern pike and the finesse of perch.

SERVES 4

1 bunch celery, chopped (do not peel)	1 tablespoon sweet butter
6 tablespoons heavy cream	2 tablespoons water
Four 7-ounce pike fillets	
Pinch celery salt	*garnish* Celery Julienne (page 197)

Put 1^1/2 cups celery in a saucepan and cover with water. Cook over medium-high heat until liquid is reduced by three-fourths. Strain the mixture through a fine mesh strainer, pressing on the solids to extract all the liquid. Put the remaining celery through a juice extractor. You should have 1^1/2 cups of juice.

Whip 2 tablespoons cream until thick; set aside. Combine ^{1}/2 cup of the strained celery reduction with the remaining ^{1}/4 cup cream in a saucepan. Cook over medium-high heat until reduced by three-fourths.

Season the pike fillets with celery salt. Arrange them in a single layer in a pan with the butter and water and cook over low heat for 4 minutes. Turn the fillets over and cook for 2 minutes longer.

Combine the raw celery juice with the celery-cream mixture and bring to a boil. Add the whipped cream and a pinch of celery salt. Bring to a boil.

Transfer the fish to warmed serving plates. Top with fried celery and pour the sauce around each serving of fish.

Cod with Pink Radish Juices

Cod is, to my taste, the finest American fish. It is harvested off the northeastern coast and is so plentiful that Portuguese fisherman travel the Atlantic to fish near our shores. Cod is not to be confused with Boston scrod, which is simply baby cod. Cod is thicker, and more subtle in its flavor and texture. Prepare the radish juice at the very last moment. It will discolor if made ahead of time.

SERVES 4

2 pounds radishes (5 cups)	Salt and cayenne pepper to taste
4 tablespoons sweet butter	2 tablespoons chopped chervil or radish greens
Four 7-ounce cod fillets	

Slice 1 cup of the radishes into very thin coins. Blanch them for 20 seconds in boiling salted water. Quickly refresh them under cold running water. Drain and set aside.

Melt 2 tablespoons butter in a medium sauté pan over medium-high heat. Add the fish and sauté 3 minutes per side. Remove and dry lightly with paper toweling. Season with salt and pepper. Put the remaining radishes through a juice extractor. You should have 2 cups of juice. (Do not juice the radishes ahead of time.) Bring the radish juice to a boil over medium-low heat and whisk in the remaining butter. Season with salt and cayenne pepper and add the chervil. Divide the sauce among 4 soup plates. Center a fillet in each plate and arrange radish coins over the fish to look like fish scales.

Black Bass with
Beet Juice and Caviar

Black bass is one of the most refined white-fleshed fishes. I don't season the fillets, just the sauce,
and the naturally sharp flavor of the caviar adds a note of its own. The subtlety of the bass and caviar
is balanced perfectly by the sweetness of the beet juice. You can use any type of black caviar you wish.
I advise against beluga, though, as it should be reserved for special occasions
where it can be enjoyed without any accompaniment.

SERVES 4

5 medium beets, peeled and chopped	Four 7-ounce black bass fillets
1 tablespoon fresh lime juice	2 ounces caviar
5 tablespoons sweet butter	
Salt and freshly ground pepper to taste	*garnish* Beet Chips (page 197)
2 teaspoons chopped chives	

Put the cut-up beets through a juice extractor. You should have 1 1/4 cups of juice.

In a small saucepan, heat the juice over medium-high heat until boiling. Reduce it by half. Add the lime juice and whisk in 3 tablespoons butter. Bring just to a boil and remove from heat. Season with salt and pepper. Add the chives.

Arrange the fillets in a single layer in a pan with enough water to reach halfway up the fish. Add the remaining 2 tablespoons butter and cook over low heat for 4 minutes. Turn the fillets over and cook for 2 minutes longer. Carefully drain the fillets and dry lightly with paper toweling.

Place the fish on warmed serving plates. Top with caviar and Beet Chips. Spoon some of the sauce around each serving of fish.

Crab Cakes
with Broccoli Juice

The natural starch in potato binds the cod cakes on page 50. Here, egg yolk binds the moist pieces of crab together. You can use ordinary mayonnaise if you don't have time to prepare the shellfish oil.

SERVES 4

1 egg yolk	2 cups unseasoned breadcrumbs, fresh or commercial
1/2 cup Lobster Oil (page 41) or Shrimp Oil (page 42)	2 heads broccoli, 4 florets reserved for garnish
1 pound crabmeat, picked over for cartilage	5 tablespoons sweet butter
1 tablespoon chopped tarragon	1 teaspoon fresh lemon juice
Salt and cayenne pepper to taste	1/4 teaspoon sugar

In a medium bowl, lightly whisk the egg yolk. Add the Lobster Oil in a thin stream, whisking constantly until the mixture thickens to the consistency of mayonnaise. Add the crabmeat, tarragon, salt, and cayenne pepper and mix well. Shape the mixture into small cakes, 2 inches in diameter. Coat them with breadcrumbs. Cover and refrigerate for 1 hour.

Put the broccoli through a juice extractor. You should have 2 cups of juice. In a small saucepan, heat the broccoli juice over medium-low heat. Whisk in 3 tablespoons butter, lemon juice, sugar, salt, and cayenne pepper. Bring to a boil and remove from heat. Keep warm. Blanch the reserved florets in boiling salted water. Drain and immediately refresh under cold running water. Drain and set aside.

In a large sauté pan, melt the remaining 2 tablespoons butter over medium heat. Add the crab cakes and sauté until golden brown on both sides, about 3 minutes per side. Divide the crab cakes among warmed serving plates and pour some of the sauce around them. Garnish with the broccoli florets.

Sea Scallops
with Zucchini Juice

This was one of my first vegetable juice recipes. It is a light version of a Provençal dish traditionally
made with zucchini, garlic, thyme, and browned butter in the place of olive oil.
A serving of four scallops, rather than eight, makes an ample appetizer.

SERVES 4

4 large zucchini, washed but not peeled, cut into chunks	$1/4$ teaspoon whole thyme leaves plus 4 sprigs thyme for garnish
3 tablespoons extra virgin olive oil	Salt and cayenne pepper to taste
$1/4$ teaspoon minced garlic	32 large sea scallops, 4 shells reserved if possible

Put the zucchini through a juice extractor. You should have 2 cups of juice. Set aside.

In a saucepan, heat 1 tablespoon olive oil until hot. Add the garlic and sauté over medium heat until translucent. Reduce the heat to medium-low and add the zucchini juice and thyme leaves. Bring to a boil and remove from heat. Whisk in the remaining 2 tablespoons olive oil. Season with salt and cayenne pepper. Keep warm.

Heat a nonstick pan over medium-high heat. When it is hot, add the scallops and sauté 20 seconds per side. Season with salt and cayenne pepper.

If serving the scallops in shells, pour a small mound of salt in the center of each serving plate to anchor each shell. Put 8 scallops into each shell (or shallow soup plate). Pour the sauce over the scallops. Garnish with thyme sprigs.

Sea Scallops in Leek Juice

This leek "juice" isn't extracted; it would be very sharp. Instead, the leeks are briefly cooked, then puréed.

SERVES 4

1/2 medium leek, chopped, including some of the green (1 cup)[*]	1 pound fresh wild mushrooms (chanterelles or morels)
4 tablespoons sweet butter	32 large sea scallops
Salt and freshly ground pepper to taste	*garnish* 4 Leek Baskets (page 198)

Cook the leeks in 1 cup boiling salted water until tender, about 3 minutes. Drain leeks and reserve cooking liquid. Put the leeks in a blender with 1 tablespoon butter and blend until smooth. Put the leek purée and 1/2 cup of the cooking liquid in a clean saucepan. Season with salt and pepper. Keep warm.

Clean and quarter the mushrooms. In a large sauté pan, melt 1 tablespoon butter over medium-high heat. Add the mushrooms and sauté until their liquid evaporates. Season with salt and pepper.

In another pan, melt the remaining 2 tablespoons butter over medium-high heat. Add the scallops and sauté 20 seconds per side. Divide the scallops among warmed serving plates. Pour some sauce around the scallops. Put the sautéed mushrooms in each leek basket and place next to scallops.

[*]*Wash leeks very thoroughly before cooking them. To help rid them of sand, trim the root end from each and then cut 2 deep crosswise slits. Rinse under cold running water.*

Shrimp in Spicy Carrot Juice

The shrimp may be steamed (page 94) rather than sautéed, if you prefer.
The seasoning has the same subtle piquancy of a spiced carrot cake; for a livelier version,
add 1 teaspoon good-quality curry powder to the sauce. Remember, if the sauce starts to separate,
whisk it over a low flame and it will come together again.

SERVES 4

10 medium carrots, peeled	1 teaspoon fresh lemon juice
32 large shrimp (about 2 pounds)	6 tablespoons sweet butter
A pinch each of ground cinnamon, ground clove, ground nutmeg, salt, and cayenne pepper	2 tablespoons chopped chervil
	garnish Carrot Julienne (page 197)

Put the carrots through a juice extractor. You should have 2 cups of juice. Peel and devein shrimp, leaving the tails intact.

In a saucepan, combine the carrot juice, spices, and lemon juice. Whisk in 4 tablespoons butter. Bring to a boil and remove from heat. Keep warm.

In a large sauté pan, melt the remaining 2 tablespoons butter over medium-high heat. Add the shrimp and sauté 1 1/2 minutes per side until thoroughly pink. Season with salt and cayenne pepper.

Arrange 8 shrimp in each of 4 soup plates and pour sauce over them. Garnish with a little chopped chervil and Carrot Julienne.

Lamb Cannelloni with Zucchini Juice

SERVES 4

1 medium eggplant	Salt and freshly ground pepper to taste
3/4 cup extra virgin olive oil	2 racks of lamb, loins removed and trimmings saved (total weight of loins about 1 pound)
1/2 green bell pepper, seeded, deribbed, and diced	
1/2 red bell pepper, seeded, deribbed, and diced	4 spring roll or egg roll wrappers*
2 anchovies, chopped	3 medium zucchini, unpeeled, cut into chunks
2 medium button mushrooms, diced	1 tablespoon whole thyme leaves
1/4 teaspoon minced garlic	2 tablespoons freshly grated Parmesan cheese

Heat the oven to 550°F. Roast the eggplant whole with olive oil for 1/2 hour. Remove from oven and reserve oil. (Leave the oven on.) Cut in half and scrape the flesh into a bowl; discard skin. Sauté the peppers, anchovies, mushrooms, and garlic in 1 tablespoon reserved oil until soft. Add the eggplant, salt, and pepper. Cook over medium-high heat for 10 minutes.

Chop the lamb trimmings. Sauté in 2 tablespoons reserved oil until golden and season with salt and pepper. Add to the eggplant mixture.

Cook the spring roll wrappers in boiling salted water until soft, about 15 seconds. Drain on paper toweling. Place 1 1/2 to 2 tablespoons of the eggplant mixture on each wrapper. Roll the wrappers around the filling into cannelloni shapes.

Put the zucchini through a juice extractor. You should have 1 cup of juice. In a saucepan, combine the zucchini juice with 6 tablespoons reserved oil and thyme leaves. Bring to a boil and remove from heat. Keep warm.

*Spring roll and egg roll wrappers are available in Oriental markets. The spring roll cannelloni are lighter than those made conventionally with pasta. If you wish, follow the directions on page 122 to use rice paper rather than spring roll wrappers.

In a medium sauté pan, heat 2 tablespoons reserved oil over medium-high heat until hot. Add the lamb loins and sauté until brown on both sides, about 1 minute per side. Remove the lamb to an oven-proof dish and finish cooking in the oven for 6 minutes.

Sprinkle the cannelloni with the cheese and put them under a preheated broiler until the cheese melts and is golden brown.

Season the lamb with salt and pepper and slice it. Divide the lamb and cannelloni among 4 warmed serving plates. Spoon some sauce around the lamb.

Lobster with Asparagus Juice

This dish contrasts sea and earth. Asparagus has great natural acidity, and the color
and flavor of the juice perfectly complement the richness of lobster.

SERVES 4

1 1/2 pounds asparagus, trimmed but not peeled	6 tablespoons sweet butter
4 one-and-a-half-pound lobsters	Salt and cayenne pepper to taste
4 asparagus spears, trimmed and peeled	*garnish* Asparagus Peelings (page 197)

Put the unpeeled asparagus through a juice extractor. You should have 1 cup of juice.

Blanch the lobsters in boiling salted water for 2 minutes; drain. Remove the meat from the tails and claws. Cut each tail into 5 medallions. Set aside.

Cook the asparagus spears in boiling salted water just until tender. Using the asparagus like brochettes, thread 5 lobster medallions on each spear. In a large sauté pan, melt 2 tablespoons butter over medium-high heat. Add the brochettes and claws and sauté for 2 minutes. Season with salt and cayenne pepper.

In a medium saucepan, combine the asparagus juice, the remaining 4 tablespoons butter, salt, and cayenne pepper over medium-low heat. Bring to a boil, then remove from the heat. Keep warm.

Arrange 1 lobster brochette and 2 claws on each of 4 warmed serving plates. Pour the sauce around the lobster and garnish with Asparagus Peelings.

Veal with Celery Juice
and Roquefort Cheese

Celery and Roquefort are a classic marriage that perfectly complements the subtle flavor of veal.
For sautés I recommend seasoning meat only after it has cooked, but roasting is a different story.

SERVES 4

4 tablespoons sweet butter	1 bunch celery, cut into pieces
2 tablespoons crumbled Roquefort cheese	2 tablespoons chopped chives
30-ounce saddle of veal	Celery salt to taste
Salt and freshly ground pepper to taste	
2 cups whole chanterelles or quartered shiitake mushrooms, washed thoroughly	*garnish* Celeriac Chips (page 197) Celery Leaves (page 197)

Heat the oven to 500°F. Combine 3 tablespoons butter and the Roquefort in a food processor or blender. Process until smooth. (If preparing in advance, refrigerate until ready to use.)

Season the veal with salt and pepper. Put the veal in a roasting pan and roast for 15 minutes (for medium doneness).

Melt the remaining 1 tablespoon butter over medium-high heat. Add the mushrooms and sauté until their liquid evaporates. Season with salt and pepper and keep warm.

Put the celery through a juice extractor. You should have about 2 cups of juice. Put the celery juice in a saucepan and bring to a boil. Remove it from the heat and whisk in the Roquefort mixture. Add the chives and celery salt.

Slice the veal and arrange it on warmed serving plates with the mushrooms. Pour the sauce around the meat and garnish with Celeriac Chips and Celery Leaves.

Chicken in Pineapple Juice

This is an exotic dish, reminiscent of the Caribbean. Pineapple can be juiced just like any vegetable;
the citrus attachment isn't necessary.

SERVES 4

1 small pineapple, peeled	3 tablespoons pine nuts
1 tablespoon freshly grated ginger	Salt and cayenne pepper to taste
1 tablespoon orange marmalade	4 whole chicken breasts, halved, skinned
4 tablespoons sweet butter	and boned
1/4 cup fresh lemon juice	

Put about half of the pineapple through a juice extractor. You should have 1 cup of juice.

Combine the pineapple juice, ginger, and marmalade in a small, nonreactive saucepan. Bring to a boil over medium-high heat and reduce by half. Remove from heat and whisk in 2 tablespoons butter and the lemon juice. Add the pine nuts and season with salt and cayenne pepper. Set aside and keep warm.

Melt the remaining 2 tablespoons butter in a large sauté pan over medium-high heat. Add the chicken and sauté 3 minutes per side. Season with salt and cayenne pepper. Divide the chicken among 4 warmed serving plates and spoon some of the sauce over the chicken.

building block
Vinaigrettes

I BEGAN TO LEARN ABOUT VINAIGRETTES IN THE FIRST YEAR OF MY
APPRENTICESHIP AT L'AUBERGE DE I'LLL. THE ESSENCE OF ANY VINAIGRETTE
IS TO COMBINE:

One part acid (vinegar, lemon juice, lime juice) to two parts oil

In order to make a vinaigrette lighter, I combine the ingredients in a
food processor or blender to create an emulsion—the oil evenly distributed
in tiny droplets throughout the mixture—and add a small amount of hot
water to bind the vinaigrette further. These two extra steps make the
vinaigrette lighter and even more flavorful than if it had simply been
whisked.

BASIC VINAIGRETTE 1

The simplest of vinaigrettes is made by combining lemon juice and olive oil.

Put 2 tablespoons fresh lemon juice (the juice of 1 lemon) in a small food processor or blender with a pinch each of salt and freshly ground pepper.

Add $1/4$ cup extra virgin olive oil and process for 30 seconds.

Add $1^1/2$ teaspoons boiling water. Process again for 10 seconds. Serve immediately or store in a tightly covered jar or bottle in the refrigerator.

BASIC VINAIGRETTE 2

Put 2 tablespoons white wine vinegar, red wine vinegar, or Champagne vinegar in a small food processor or blender with a pinch each of salt and freshly ground pepper.

Add $1/4$ cup canola or hazelnut oil and process for 30 seconds.

Add $1^1/2$ teaspoons boiling water. Process again for 10 seconds. Serve immediately or store in a tightly covered jar or bottle in the refrigerator.

Each vinaigrette, including most of those that follow, will keep in the refrigerator for 1 week, but as always—the fresher, the better. Each of the basic vinaigrettes is perfect on any form of salad. Use 2 tablespoons vinaigrette per serving on salads, 2 to 3 tablespoons to dress simple steamed or sautéed dishes.

The recipes that follow use the concepts just explained. Use these vinaigrettes instead of heavy or complicated sauces to accompany simply cooked meats, fish, and shellfish.

GINGER VINAIGRETTE

MAKES $3/4$ CUP

$1/2$ cup extra virgin olive oil
1 tablespoon fresh lime juice
1 tablespoon sherry vinegar
1 teaspoon freshly grated ginger
Salt and freshly ground pepper to taste
1 tablespoon boiling water

Combine all ingredients except boiling water in a food processor or blender. Process for 30 seconds. With the motor running, add the water and process for 10 seconds longer. Store, tightly covered, in the refrigerator up to 1 day.

SOY AND GINGER VINAIGRETTE

MAKES 4 CUPS

$1/2$ cup soy sauce
$1/2$ cup fresh lemon juice
1 tablespoon freshly grated ginger
$1^1/2$ cups extra virgin olive oil
$1^1/2$ cups canola oil
Salt and freshly ground pepper to taste
6 tablespoons boiling water

Combine all ingredients except boiling water in a food processor or blender. Process for 30 seconds. With the motor running, add the water and process for 10 seconds longer. Store, tightly covered, in the refrigerator up to 1 week.

BASIL VINAIGRETTE

MAKES 1 1/2 CUPS

1 cup extra virgin olive oil
1 tablespoon fresh lemon juice
1 tablespoon sherry vinegar
12 large basil leaves
Salt and freshly ground pepper to taste
2 tablespoons boiling water

Combine all ingredients except boiling water in a food processor or blender. Process for 1 minute. With the motor running, add the water and process for 10 seconds longer. Store, tightly covered, in the refrigerator 1 day.

note *After one day, Basil Vinaigrette loses its pretty, clear green color. The flavor, though, will still be very nice for several days.*

CITRUS VINAIGRETTE

MAKES 1 1/2 CUPS

1/2 cup extra virgin olive oil
1 tablespoon sherry vinegar
3 tablespoons soy sauce
Pinch cayenne pepper
2 pinches celery salt
1 drop Tabasco

2 tablespoons boiling water
1/2 lime
1 lemon
1/4 pink grapefruit
1/2 orange
10 pink peppercorns
1 tablespoon fresh ginger julienne
1 bunch cilantro, stems discarded and leaves cut into ribbons
Salt and freshly ground pepper to taste

Combine the oil, vinegar, soy sauce, cayenne pepper, celery salt, and Tabasco in a food processor or blender. Process for 30 seconds. With the motor running, add the water and process for 30 seconds longer. Transfer the mixture to a bowl and set aside.

Peel the fruits and remove the sections. Cut into small dice (reserve the juice).

Add the diced fruit to the bowl of vinaigrette with a teaspoon of each juice. Stir in the peppercorns, ginger, and cilantro. Adjust seasoning with salt and pepper. Store, tightly covered, in the refrigerator up to 1 day. Or, prepare the vinaigrette base up to 1 week in advance and add the fruits, peppercorns, ginger, and cilantro just before serving.

CURRY VINAIGRETTE

MAKES 2 CUPS

1/2 cup Curry Oil (page 39)
1/2 cup sherry vinegar
Salt and freshly ground pepper to taste
1 tablespoon boiling water
1/2 medium apple, peeled and diced
1/2 medium banana, diced

Combine the oil, vinegar, salt, and pepper in a food processor or blender. Process for 30 seconds. With the motor running, add the water and process for 10 seconds longer. Transfer the mixture to a bowl and stir in the diced apple and banana. Store, tightly covered, in the refrigerator up to 1 day. Or, prepare the vinaigrette base up to 1 week in advance and add the chopped apple and banana just before serving.

HAZELNUT VINAIGRETTE

MAKES 1/2 CUP

2 tablespoons hazelnut oil
2 tablespoons canola oil
2 tablespoons sherry vinegar
1 1/2 teaspoons boiling water
1 shallot, peeled and chopped
1 leek, white part only,
washed thoroughly and chopped
Salt and freshly ground pepper to taste

Combine the oils and vinegar in a food processor or blender. Process for 30 seconds. With the motor running, add the water and process for 10 seconds longer. In a mixing bowl, combine shallot and leek. Add the vinaigrette and mix well. Season with salt and pepper. Store, tightly covered, in the refrigerator up to 1 week.

JUNIPER VINAIGRETTE

MAKES 1 CUP

1 tablespoon juniper berries
1 shallot, peeled and chopped
2 tablespoons sherry vinegar

1 tablespoon gin
2 tablespoons canola oil
2 tablespoons walnut oil
Salt and freshly ground pepper to taste
1 1/2 teaspoons boiling water
1 bunch chives, chopped

Combine all ingredients except boiling water and chives in a food processor or blender. Process for 30 seconds. With the motor running, add the water and process for 1 minute longer. Stir in the chives. Store, tightly covered, in the refrigerator for up to 1 week.

PEANUT VINAIGRETTE

MAKES 2 1/2 CUPS

1 cup peanut oil[*]
3/4 cup canola oil
3/4 cup sherry vinegar
1 small leek, white part only,
washed thoroughly and chopped
2 small shallots, peeled and chopped
Salt and freshly ground pepper to taste
3 1/2 tablespoons boiling water

Combine all ingredients except boiling water in a food processor or blender. Process for 30 seconds. With the motor running, add the water and process for 10 seconds longer. Store, tightly covered, in the refrigerator up to 1 week.

*If you can find oil pressed from roasted peanuts, by all means use it. It is darker in color than oil from unroasted peanuts and has a more pronounced peanut flavor.

TRUFFLE VINAIGRETTE

MAKES 1 1/2 CUPS

1 cup canola oil
2 tablespoons fresh lemon juice
1 tablespoon sherry vinegar
3 tablespoons truffle juice*
Salt and freshly ground pepper to taste
2 tablespoons boiling water

Combine all ingredients except boiling water in a food processor or blender. Process for 30 seconds. With the motor running, add the water and process for 1 minute longer. Store, tightly covered, in the refrigerator 1 week.

Truffle juice can be purchased in cans in specialty stores and gourmet markets. As you can see, a little goes a long way. You may also use the liquid in which jarred or canned truffles are packed.

LOBSTER OR SHRIMP VINAIGRETTE

MAKES 1 CUP

2 tablespoons Champagne or white wine vinegar
1/4 cup Lobster Oil (page 41) or
Shrimp Oil (page 42)
1 tablespoon Dijon mustard
1/4 cup fresh lemon juice
Salt and freshly ground pepper to taste
1 1/2 teaspoons boiling water
2 tablespoons capers
2 tablespoons chives cut into 1/2-inch lengths

Combine all ingredients except boiling water, capers, and chives in a food processor or blender. Process for 30 seconds. With the motor running, add the water and process for 1 minute longer. Stir in the capers and chives just before serving. Store, tightly covered, in the refrigerator up to 1 week.

Buckwheat Pasta
with Black Bass and Caviar

This recipe is inspired by the famous Russian dish of buckwheat blini with sturgeon and caviar.
The buckwheat pasta is quite easy, but if you don't want to make it yourself, buy fresh pasta.
In a pinch, boxed dried lasagne noodles will do nicely. This is a very festive dish for a special occasion.

SERVES 4

Buckwheat Pasta (recipe follows)
3 tablespoons sweet butter
1 shallot, peeled and chopped
1 cup dry white wine
1 cup Mixed Vegetable Broth (page 68)
1 cup heavy cream
1/2 cucumber, finely julienned

4 large white button mushrooms, finely
  julienned
Salt and freshly ground pepper to taste
1 pound black bass fillets, cut into 2 × 4-
  inch pieces
Caviar Vinaigrette (recipe follows)

Prepare the Buckwheat Pasta.

In a medium saucepan, melt 1 tablespoon butter over medium-high heat. Add the shallot and cook until translucent. Add the wine and cook until evaporated. Add the Mixed Vegetable Broth and reduce by half. Add the cream, cucumber, and mushrooms. Season with salt and pepper. Cook until thickened. Keep warm.

Melt the remaining 2 tablespoons butter in a sauté pan. Arrange the pieces of fish in a single layer in the butter and cook over medium-high heat for 3 minutes. Turn the fish over and cook 3 minutes longer or until desired doneness.

Cook the pasta for 45 seconds to 1 minute in boiling salted water. Drain. Combine all ingredients for the Caviar Vinaigrette and set it aside.

Fan 3 pieces of pasta alternately with 2 pieces of fish on each of 4 serving plates. Spoon some of the sauce over each and pour Caviar Vinaigrette around the fish.

Buckwheat Pasta

$3/4$ cup buckwheat flour
Scant $1/2$ cup all-purpose flour
1 egg
1 egg yolk
1 tablespoon extra virgin olive oil
1 tablespoon milk
Pinch of salt

Combine all ingredients by hand or in a food processor or blender to form a dough. Knead briefly. Cover and let rest in the refrigerator for at least $1/2$ hour. Roll it out to $1/8$-inch thickness with a rolling pin on a lightly floured surface or run it through a pasta machine. Cut the pasta into small rectangles, 2×4 inches. Cover with plastic wrap and refrigerate until needed.

Caviar Vinaigrette

2 tablespoons sherry vinegar
3 tablespoons safflower or grapeseed oil
2 tablespoons caviar (sevruga if possible)
Salt and freshly ground pepper to taste

Combine all ingredients and set aside.

Salmon in Rice Paper
with Citrus Vinaigrette

Several sprigs flat-leaf parsley	1 tablespoon canola oil
Four 6-ounce skinless salmon fillets (about $3 \times 1^1/2 \times 1$ inch)	1 tablespoon sweet butter
Four 8-inch sheets rice paper	$^1/_2$ cup Citrus Vinaigrette (page 17)

Heat the oven to 425°F. Press 2 or 3 parsley leaves onto one side of each fillet.

Soften each round of rice paper between layers of damp kitchen toweling for about 5 minutes until pliable enough to roll without cracking but not wet.

Wrap each fillet in rice paper: Place it about 2 inches from the bottom of the circle. Bring the bottom over the fillet, then roll the fillet to enclose it. Trim the sides off until even with the salmon.

In a medium nonstick pan, heat the oil and butter over medium-high heat until hot. Add the salmon packages and sauté $1^1/2$ minutes per side until rice paper is crisp. Transfer to an oven-proof dish, put in the oven and cook for 2 minutes. Remove from the oven, cover and let rest for 1 minute.

Slice each package into 3 pieces. Arrange the slices on warmed serving plates. Serve with Citrus Vinaigrette.

Skate Wings with Artichokes

Lobster or Shrimp Vinaigrette, together with the artichokes, provides just the right amount of acidity to balance skate, one of the more gelatinous or fatty fishes. If you are pressed for time, you may use frozen (thawed) artichoke hearts here.

SERVES 4

8 medium artichokes	Canola oil, for frying
2 tablespoons fresh lemon juice	1 tablespoon all-purpose flour
3 tablespoons extra virgin olive oil	2 tablespoons sweet butter
1 medium onion, peeled and sliced	1 pound skate wing fillets
2 cups dry white wine	1/2 cup Lobster or Shrimp Vinaigrette (page 19)
Salt and freshly ground pepper to taste	

Trim artichoke hearts as directed on page 69. Put the hearts in a bowl of water acidulated with lemon juice (to keep them from discoloring).

Heat the olive oil in a nonreactive saucepan and sauté the onion until translucent. Add 6 of the artichoke hearts and the wine. Cook over medium heat until hearts are tender. Put the hearts in a food processor or blender with 2 tablespoons cooking liquid and process to a smooth purée. Season with salt and pepper and set aside.

Heat the canola oil (1 inch deep) until very hot (350° to 375°F). Drain the 2 remaining artichoke hearts and pat dry. Cut them into matchstick pieces. Flour them lightly and fry until golden brown and crisp. Drain on paper toweling and salt lightly.

Heat the butter in a sauté pan. Add the skate and cook over medium-high heat 20 seconds per side. Season with salt and pepper.

Place the skate on warmed serving plates. Spoon some artichoke purée down the center of each fillet and top with the fried artichoke matchsticks. Pour some Lobster or Shrimp Vinaigrette around the skate.

Salmon Cabbage
with Juniper Vinaigrette

This is my version of the classic stuffed cabbage. The juniper berry is very pungent and goes extremely well with cabbage. You can prepare the salmon and cabbage rolls in the morning or even the night before, then slice and sauté them at the last minute.

SERVES 4

1 savoy cabbage (or any other cabbage if savoy is unavailable)

$1^1/2$ pounds salmon fillets, sliced $^1/3$ inch thick

2 tablespoons canola oil

$^1/2$ cup Juniper Vinaigrette (page 18)

12 stalks chives, cut into 2-inch lengths

2 tablespoons salmon roe

garnish 12 Gaufrette Potatoes (page 47), homemade potato chips, or even good-quality potato chips straight from the bag

Core the cabbage and carefully separate the leaves. Blanch the leaves for 1 minute in boiling salted water. Quickly refresh them in a bowl of ice water. Drain and pat dry.

Lay a piece of aluminum foil approximately 8 × 10 inches on a work surface. Cover the foil with cabbage leaves. Cover cabbage completely with salmon. Lift the edge of the foil on the long side and, with a spatula, roll cabbage and salmon into a tight cylinder. Roll tightly in the foil. Twist the ends of the foil tightly. Refrigerate for at least 2 hours.

Unwrap the rolled salmon and cut into 1-inch slices. Heat canola oil in a sauté pan and cook the slices over medium-high heat 30 seconds per side.

Arrange 3 slices on each of 4 serving plates. Sprinkle with Juniper Vinaigrette and garnish with Gaufrette Potatoes, chives and roe.

Salad of Crayfish, Zucchini, and Tomato

This is a fresh salad without lettuce. Shrimp works just as well as crayfish, is less expensive and more plentiful. If you can find crayfish from New Orleans or the West Coast, by all means try them.

SERVES 4

48 whole crayfish or 24 medium shrimp, peeled and deveined

2 medium zucchini

2 tablespoons extra virgin olive oil

1 medium onion, peeled and chopped

2 cloves garlic, peeled and chopped

4 medium tomatoes, peeled, seeded, and coarsely chopped

1/2 bunch fresh thyme, tied into a bundle with kitchen string

Salt and freshly ground pepper to taste

1/2 cup Basil Vinaigrette (page 17)

garnish   4 sprigs basil

Following the directions on page 94 for shrimp, steam the crayfish for 5 minutes, then let cool. Separate the tails from the bodies. Remove the tail meat and discard the shells and bodies. (If using shrimp, steam as directed on page 94 for 5 minutes; set aside.)

Slice the zucchini into thin coins and blanch them in boiling salted water for 1 minute. Drain and refresh under cold running water.

Heat the olive oil over medium-high heat and sauté the onion and garlic until translucent. Add the tomatoes and thyme and cook for 15 minutes, stirring occasionally. Remove and discard the thyme. Set the mixture aside to cool.

Season the zucchini, crayfish, and tomatoes individually with salt and pepper. Pour the Basil Vinaigrette over the tomatoes and stir well.

On each of 4 serving plates, overlap zucchini slices to form a large ring. Arrange crayfish within the rings. Spoon the tomato mixture around the zucchini and garnish with basil sprigs.

Cold Sea Urchin Soufflé

SERVES 8

1 generous cup sea urchins*	1 cup heavy cream, whipped
1 cup Mixed Vegetable Broth (page 68)	1/4 teaspoon fresh lemon juice
2 egg yolks	Salt and cayenne pepper to taste
1/2 teaspoon unflavored gelatin	1/2 cup Ginger Vinaigrette (page 16)

Press the sea urchins through a fine sieve to obtain a purée. In a medium saucepan, combine the sea urchin purée, Mixed Vegetable Broth, and egg yolks. Heat gently over low heat, whisking constantly, until lukewarm. Sprinkle the gelatin over the mixture and cook, whisking constantly, until gelatin is dissolved and mixture is hot and slightly thickened. (Do not let the mixture boil, or the egg yolks will scramble.)

Transfer the mixture to a mixing bowl set in a larger bowl filled with ice water. Gently stir the mixture as it cools. When it is cool to the touch and has thickened, remove the bowl from the ice water and fold in the whipped cream. Season with lemon juice, salt, and cayenne pepper.

Pour into espresso-size cups or 2-ounce ramekins. Cover tightly and refrigerate until set, at least 1 hour.

When ready to serve, unmold each soufflé by dipping the cup into hot water and running a knife around the inside of the cup. Invert onto a small serving plate. Serve with a drizzle of Ginger Vinaigrette.

*Sea urchin (uni in Japanese) may be obtained at Japanese grocers, from some Japanese restaurants, and some fishmongers. The distinctive flavor of sea urchin comes through most clearly when eaten cold and uncooked. This may be too much for the less adventuresome, so I created this dish which gentles the flavor with cooking, then cools to a soufflé. Serve these little soufflés with the wonderfully crisp Rice Crackers on page 157.

Steamed Shrimp with
Champagne Vinaigrette

*This warm salad combines hot shrimp with cooling greens and a tangy Champagne vinaigrette.
Warm salads eventually became popular in France, but it seems to me no one understood the marriage
of such diverse elements better than my mentor, Louis Outhier, who always featured warm salads
on his seasonal menu at L'Oasis in La Napoule.*

SERVES 4

3 tablespoons sweet butter

1 medium shallot, peeled and finely
  chopped

1/2 cup Champagne or white wine
  vinegar

1/2 cup heavy cream

Salt and cayenne pepper to taste

24 large shrimp, peeled and deveined

2 cups mixed salad greens

1 medium avocado

4 medium button mushrooms, caps very
  thinly sliced and stems julienned

1 medium tomato, peeled, seeded, and
  diced

1/2 cup Soy and Ginger Vinaigrette
  (page 16)

In a medium saucepan, melt 1 tablespoon butter over medium-high heat and sauté the
shallot until translucent. Add the vinegar and cook until reduced by half. Add the cream and
cook until reduced by half. Whisk in the remaining 2 tablespoons butter, bring to a boil and
immediately remove from heat. Season with salt and cayenne pepper and keep warm.

Steam the shrimp as directed on page 94 until they are pink throughout, 3 to 4 minutes.
Season with salt and cayenne pepper.

While the shrimp are cooking, arrange the greens on each of 4 serving plates. Peel and
cut the avocado into thin slices. Place 2 or 3 slices of avocado on the greens on each plate.
Scatter mushrooms over them and top with a small spoonful of diced tomato. Drizzle with 2
tablespoons Soy and Ginger Vinaigrette. Arrange the shrimp around the greens and spoon
some of the Champagne vinegar sauce over them.

Open Ravioli with Shrimp

Reminiscent of lasagne, this dish is more precisely known as "open ravioli." It always struck me that shrimp, lobster, scallops, and other delicate ravioli fillings frequently overcook, as the boiling of the pasta controls the cooking of the filling. Here, the pasta and the shrimp are cooked separately. There is no limit to the different fillings you can use. Let your imagination know no bounds. If you don't want to make your own pasta, trim fresh or cooked, dried lasagne noodles.

SERVES 4

5 tablespoons sweet butter

24 large shrimp, peeled and deveined

2 medium shallots, peeled and chopped

1 clove garlic, peeled and chopped

1 cup dry white wine

2 tablespoons chopped parsley

Salt and freshly ground pepper to taste

Pasta (recipe follows), prepared 1 day in advance

1/2 cup Lobster or Shrimp Vinaigrette (page 19)

In a large sauté pan, melt 3 tablespoons butter over medium-high heat and sauté the shrimp for 1 minute on each side. Add the shallots and garlic and cook for about 20 seconds. Deglaze the pan with the wine. Remove the shrimp from the pan and keep warm. Reduce the liquid in the pan by one-third. Whisk in the remaining 2 tablespoons butter. Add the parsley and shrimp and season with salt and pepper. Set aside and keep warm.

Cook the pasta in boiling salted water for 15 seconds. Drain immediately and lightly pat dry.

Place one unmarked sheet of pasta on each of 4 serving plates. Put 6 shrimp and some sauce on each square of pasta, then cover with a sheet of "parsley printed" pasta. Sprinkle Lobster Vinaigrette around the plate.

Pasta

2 cups all-purpose flour
3 eggs
1 teaspoon white wine vinegar
Pinch salt
4 flat-leaf parsley leaves

Mix the flour, eggs, vinegar, and salt in a food processor or by hand until very well combined. Cover and let rest in the refrigerator overnight. Roll out the pasta by hand or use a pasta machine until paper thin. Cut out eight 2-inch squares. Decorate 4 of the sheets with a parsley leaf, pressing the leaves into the dough so they adhere.

Lobster Couscous

This is a memorable salad, served at room temperature. If you like, you can shape the couscous

for each serving in individual savarin (ring) molds. Pack it down firmly, then turn it out.

I would arrange lobster medallions in the center with a claw on either side.

SERVES 4

1 medium carrot, chopped	4 mint leaves, cut into ribbons
1/2 medium leek, white part only, washed thoroughly and chopped	4 basil leaves, cut into ribbons
1/2 medium onion, chopped	2 medium tomatoes, peeled, seeded, and chopped
1 stalk celery, chopped	1 medium cucumber, peeled, seeded, and chopped
1 Bouquet Garni (page 196)	1/2 cup diced pitted ripe olives
Four 1-pound lobsters	Salt and freshly ground pepper to taste
1/4 teaspoon harissa pepper or Chinese chili paste	1 cup Ginger Vinaigrette (page 16)
2/3 cup extra virgin olive oil	2 tablespoons chopped chervil
1 cup couscous	

Add the carrot, leek, onion, celery, and Bouquet Garni to a large pot of water and bring to a rolling boil. Add the lobsters and cook for 10 minutes. Remove the lobsters from the broth. Strain and reserve 1 3/4 cups of the broth. Carefully remove the lobster meat; cut each tail into 5 medallions and leave the claws whole. Set aside in a large bowl.

Put the reserved broth in a medium saucepan with harissa pepper and olive oil. Whisk over medium-high heat until hot. Pour over the couscous. Let the couscous sit for 20 minutes, without stirring, until it has absorbed nearly all of the liquid. Gently stir in the mint, basil, tomatoes, cucumber, and olives.

Season the lobster with salt and pepper. Add enough Ginger Vinaigrette to coat, turning gently. Divide the couscous among 4 serving plates. Arrange 5 medallions and 2 claws on or around each serving. Drizzle each serving with 2 to 3 tablespoons Ginger Vinaigrette and scatter chervil over all.

Squab and Lentil Salad

This is a perfect fall and winter dish, one of my favorites. I always felt that this was a rich combination of metallic flavors: the "copper" of squab and the "iron" of lentils.

SERVES 4

1 cup dried lentils	3/4 cup Peanut Vinaigrette (page 18)
2 squab or one 2- to 3-pound baby chicken, skinned and boned	1/2 cup Mushroom Syrup (page 68)
1/4 cup cooked foie gras or chicken livers, diced	1 tablespoon sherry vinegar
	2 tablespoons peanut oil
1 tablespoon sweet butter	1 teaspoon cracked black peppercorns
Salt and freshly ground pepper to taste	1/4 cup cracked raw peanuts
1/2 cup frisée lettuce (chicory)	

Soak the lentils in cold water for 2 hours. Drain, put into a pot and cover with salted water. Bring to a boil; reduce heat and simmer until tender, about 30 minutes. Drain and set aside.

Stuff the leg meat with the cooked foie gras. Roll each leg in a piece of aluminum foil. Put the foil packages in a pot of water and bring to a boil. Immediately remove the pot from the heat and let the packages cool in the water until ready to use.

Melt the butter over medium-high heat and sauté the breasts 2 minutes per side. Season with salt and pepper. Cut each breast into 4 slices.

Season the frisée lettuce with salt, pepper, and 1/4 cup of the vinaigrette. Season the lentils separately with salt, pepper, and the remaining vinaigrette.

Warm the Mushroom Syrup and whisk in the vinegar and peanut oil.

Mound some of the frisée in the center of each serving plate. Spoon lentils on top of the frisée. Unwrap the stuffed legs and place one on each plate. Add slices of squab breast to each plate and sprinkle cracked black pepper and peanuts over all. Pour some of the mushroom sauce over the breast meat.

Beef on a String
with Basil Vinaigrette

This is my version of a fast pot-au-feu, or boiled dinner. Have your butcher cut the sirloin for you, very thin as for Japanese sukiyaki. If you follow the directions carefully, the vegetables will be crisp-tender and the meat moist and flavorful.

SERVES 4

2 medium carrots, peeled
2 long turnips, peeled
2 medium zucchini
8 string beans, trimmed
8 pencil-thin stalks asparagus, trimmed
 and peeled

12 thin slices prime sirloin, about $5 \times 1^{1}/2$ inches and no more than $^{1}/4$ inch thick
Salt and freshly ground pepper to taste
1 quart Vegetable Broth (recipe follows)
Basil Vinaigrette with Vegetables (recipe follows)

Put the carrots, turnips, and zucchini into matchstick pieces about $2^{1}/2$ inches long. Cook the vegetables in boiling salted water until tender, zucchini 30 seconds, carrots, beans, turnips, and asparagus $1^{1}/2$ to 2 minutes.

Lay sirloin slices on a flat surface. Season with salt and pepper. Divide vegetables among the meat slices and roll the meat around them. Secure each roll with kitchen string.

Heat the broth until boiling. Place the meat rolls in the broth and poach them for 40 seconds. Remove them immediately. Cut off the string. Serve with Basil Vinaigrette with Vegetables.

Vegetable Broth

1 tablespoon extra virgin olive oil
1 tablespoon sweet butter
1 medium carrot, peeled and diced
1 bulb fennel, diced
5 leeks, white part only, washed thoroughly and sliced
10 shallots, peeled and chopped
10 cloves garlic, peeled and chopped
$1/4$ cup chopped chervil
$1/2$ cup chopped dill
2 cups dry white wine
$1/4$ teaspoon cracked coriander seed
$1/4$ teaspoon cracked black pepper
$3 1/2$ cups water

In a medium pot, heat the olive oil and butter over medium-high heat. Add the vegetables and cook until soft. Add the herbs, wine, coriander seed, and pepper. Cook until the wine evaporates. Add the water and cook for 20 minutes. Strain through a fine mesh strainer, pressing on the solids to extract as much liquid as possible.

Basil Vinaigrette with Vegetables

Basil Vinaigrette (page 17)
$1/2$ medium red bell pepper, seeded, deribbed, and finely diced
$1/2$ medium zucchini, finely diced
$1/2$ medium tomato, peeled, seeded, and finely diced
1 clove garlic, peeled and finely chopped
2 shallots, peeled and finely chopped
$1/2$ teaspoon chopped chives
$1/2$ teaspoon chopped parsley
$1/2$ teaspoon chopped tarragon
$1/2$ teaspoon chopped dill

Combine all ingredients.

Sweetbreads
with Yellow Potato Salad

Potato salad with crisp bacon is a dish that I grew up with in Alsace. Here the potatoes dominate, and we add the crispness of sautéed sweetbreads. Blanching the sweetbreads before sautéing them guarantees they will be very crisp. Use a variety of salad greens, as fresh as you can find.

SERVES 4

1 pound sweetbreads	Salt and freshly ground pepper to taste
4 medium yellow or red-skin potatoes	3/4 cup Hazelnut Vinaigrette (page 18)
All-purpose flour	1/2 pound mixed salad greens
3 tablespoons duck fat or hazelnut oil	

Blanch the sweetbreads in boiling salted water for 1 minute. Drain and let cool to room temperature. Place the cooled sweetbreads in a pan. Set another pan on top of them and weight it. Let the sweetbreads "press" for 30 minutes.

Cook the potatoes in boiling salted water until tender when pierced with a fork, about 15 minutes. Peel and slice 1/4 inch thick.

Slice the sweetbreads on the diagonal about 1/2 inch thick. Flour them lightly. In a large sauté pan, heat the duck fat over medium-high heat until very hot. Sauté sweetbreads and potatoes on both sides until golden brown and crisp, about 4 minutes. Season with salt and pepper.

Toss sweetbreads and potatoes in Hazelnut Vinaigrette.

Divide the salad greens among 4 serving plates. Arrange a circle of potatoes on the greens with the sweetbreads in the center. Sprinkle more of the vinaigrette over all.

Fresh Truffle Salad

As you probably know, truffles are very expensive whether they be fresh, canned, or jarred. I try never to use truffles unless they are fresh, in January or February. When fresh, their intensity is remarkable. This dish is a pure extravagance, but one that truly exploits the natural flavor of the truffle.

SERVES 4

2 tablespoons fresh lemon juice	2 medium black truffles (fresh only), thinly shaved
2 tablespoons extra virgin olive oil	
Salt and freshly ground pepper to taste	1 knob celeriac, peeled and finely julienned
1/2 pound mixed salad greens	

Whisk together the lemon juice, olive oil, salt, and pepper.

Place some greens on each of 4 plates. Dip the truffle slices into the olive oil dressing and arrange them in a ring around the greens. Scatter the celeriac over all and spoon some dressing over the salad.

Asparagus Salad

This is a wonderful vegetarian salad for the spring and summer. The hot asparagus and cold salad are a nice contrast, what we call a chaud-froid *in French.*

SERVES 4

1 pound asparagus, trimmed and peeled	Salt and cayenne pepper to taste
1 medium avocado	2 heads endive, leaves separated
1 tablespoon plus 1 teaspoon fresh lemon juice	1 pound mixed salad greens
2 egg yolks	Two 3-ounce packages enoki mushrooms or 8 thinly sliced button mushrooms
Pinch salt	$^1/_2$ cup Soy and Ginger Vinaigrette (page 16)
6 tablespoons water	
4 tablespoons sweet butter, softened	1 teaspoon chopped chives or parsley

Tie the asparagus in 3 bunches. Cook in boiling salted water until tender, about 5 minutes. Drain and immediately refresh under cold running water.

Peel and thinly slice the avocado. Gently toss with 1 tablespoon lemon juice and set aside.

In a double boiler set over simmering water, whisk together the egg yolks, a pinch of salt, and the water until frothy.

Beat in the soft butter and whisk until thick enough to coat a spoon. Don't let the Hollandaise curdle. Season with salt, cayenne pepper, and 1 teaspoon lemon juice.

Arrange 5 endive leaves on each of 4 serving plates to form a star. Place mixed greens in the center of each. Top with 3 slices of avocado and sprinkle with mushrooms. Dress with the vinaigrette. Top with the warm asparagus. Spoon 2 tablespoons Hollandaise over each portion of asparagus and sprinkle with chives or parsley.

Chanterelles and Spinach Salad

"Baby" spinach leaves are very tender, and their small size is so appealing.
Wash and dry the mushrooms and spinach well.

SERVES 4

1/4 cup peanut oil	1/3 cup Hazelnut Vinaigrette (page 18)
1 clove garlic, peeled and chopped	1/4 cup mixed chopped herbs (chervil, parsley, and chives)
2 shallots, peeled and chopped	
1 pound chanterelles or shiitake mushrooms, washed thoroughly	1/4 cup hazelnut or extra virgin olive oil
Salt and freshly ground pepper to taste	1 teaspoon soy sauce
1/4 pound "baby" or regular spinach, stemmed and washed thoroughly	2 tablespoons water

In a medium sauté pan, heat the peanut oil over medium-high heat. When hot, add the garlic and shallots and cook until translucent. Add the mushrooms. Season with salt and pepper. Cover and cook for 12 minutes, stirring occasionally.

Lightly pat spinach dry and toss with Hazelnut Vinaigrette. Add the chopped herbs and toss. Arrange on plates.

Add hazelnut oil, soy sauce, and water to the mushrooms. Cook, uncovered, until the cooking liquid is reduced by half. Arrange the mushrooms on the spinach and spoon over some of the sauce.

Flavored Oils

LIKE THE VEGETABLE JUICES AND THE VINAIGRETTES, THE FLAVORED OILS ARE "BUILDING BLOCKS" IN MANY OF MY RECIPES, AND THEY TOO CAN BE SERVED WITH THE QUICKLY PREPARED SAUTÉS OR STEAMED dishes of meat, poultry, fish, and shellfish found on pages 86 to 94. With any of the flavored oils on hand, a memorable—and astonishingly simple—dinner can be made in minutes.

Flavored oils can be used in as many ways as you can imagine. They provide nearly infinite inspiration when you want to dress a salad (try a vinaigrette of Mustard Oil with sherry vinegar). They make for absolutely unheard-of mayonnaises. Use them in the place of butter or oil when sautéing. You could even, if you wished, deep-fat fry in a flavored oil.

I use the oils most often, I think, to drizzle over sautéed and steamed foods, for an effect as elegant as it is simple. Don't hesitate to moisten pieces of fresh, crusty bread with it. Finally, anytime you marinate meats before grilling them, consider marinating them in one of your flavored oils (see page 185). The flavor is incomparable.

All of the flavored oils may be prepared in advance. They are as delicious served cold as when gently heated.

There are various types of oils, prepared by slightly different methods. The techniques are so simple they can be mastered the first time you make them. Whenever I use a "neutral" oil, I prefer to use canola oil (which has the lowest saturated fat content).

Ground Spice Oils	**Fresh Root Oils**	**Vegetable Juice Oils**
Herb Oils	**Fruit Oils**	**Miscellaneous Oils**

GROUND SPICE OILS

Each spice is in powdered form.

To make a spiced oil, first mix water with the ground spice before the oil is added. This rejuvenates or "wakes up" the flavor of the spice. Without this first step, the essential flavor of the spice won't reach its potential.

If you can't find caraway, cardamom, anise, or fennel in powdered form, you can grind the spices yourself in a clean electric coffee grinder, mortar and pestle, or small ("mini") food processor.

MAKES 2 CUPS

Mustard	Garlic
Paprika	Cumin
Curry	Fennel
Turmeric	Cinnamon
Ginger	Wasabi
Caraway	Anise
Cardamom	Saffron

Mix 3 tablespoons ground spice with 1 tablespoon water to a smooth paste. If the paste is very dry, add a little more water. The paste should not be liquid; the consistency of ketchup is just about right.

Put the paste in a clear jar.

Add 2 cups of canola oil.

Cover the jar tightly and shake vigorously.

Set the jar on a kitchen shelf for 2 days. You may shake the oil several times during this time to increase the strength of the oil.

The spice particles will gradually settle to the bottom of the jar. After 2 days, remove the oil on top with a ladle, being careful not to disturb the solids at the bottom too much. Discard the solids. Filter the oil—not the solids—through a paper coffee filter or a double thickness of fine cheesecloth. Do not filter the solids!

Store the spiced oil, tightly covered, in the refrigerator or at room temperature for up to 6 months.

FRESH ROOT OILS

These highly flavored fresh roots combine beautifully with oils. ("Root" is most evocative but not strictly accurate, for shallots and garlic are really bulbs, leeks are vegetables, and ginger is a rhizome.) Since the flavorings are fresh, they don't need to be mixed with water; they will "wake up" when combined with oil. Due to the individual, characteristic flavor of each, some oils complement that flavor better than others.

Because the roots are pungent and fresh, the flavored oil will be ready to use just 1 to 2 hours after mixing. These oils must be kept tightly covered in the refrigerator, where they will keep up to 2 weeks.

MAKES 2 CUPS

Shallot	Leek
Garlic	Ginger
Horseradish	

Peel the roots. If using leeks, quarter them lengthwise and rinse thoroughly; pat dry.

Mince the roots by hand or finely chop in a food processor. (If using a food processor, one of the small "mini" models is preferred. It is nearly impossible to process small amounts of garlic and the like to uniformly tiny pieces in the larger machines.)

For every 2 tablespoons of chopped root, add 2 cups of the appropriate oil:

Shallot	Canola Oil
Garlic	Extra virgin olive oil
Horseradish	Canola Oil
Ginger	Canola Oil
Leek	Walnut or hazelnut oil

Put the chopped root in a clean jar. Add oil. Cover the jar tightly and shake vigorously.

Store the root oil, tightly covered, in the refrigerator for at least 1 to 2 hours.

VEGETABLE JUICE OILS

These oils combine freshly extracted vegetable juices with oils. Every one of the vegetable juice oils may be used as a delicious sauce by itself. Bell pepper juice and beet juice may be reduced to a syrup and then combined with oil for a sauce with especially brilliant flavor and color. Vegetable juice oils are ready to use immediately.

MAKES 3 CUPS

Make 1 cup of the desired vegetable juice as described on page xii. Put the juice in a clear jar.

Add 2 cups of the appropriate oil. Combine the juices and oils as follows:

Carrot	Canola oil
Zucchini	Extra virgin olive oil
Asparagus	Canola oil
Bell Pepper	Extra virgin olive oil
Celery	Canola oil
Beet	Canola oil
Leek	Canola oil

Cover the jar tightly and shake vigorously.

Store the vegetable juice oil, tightly covered, in the refrigerator for up to 2 weeks. For an oil with uniform color, shake well before using. I prefer not to, though, as the oil is so pretty when it is "broken," the tiny pieces of vegetable color catching the light. Never filter a vegetable juice oil.

HERB OILS

These oils are flavored with fresh herbs only. There are 2 types of herb oils, those made with tender, mild herbs and those made with stronger herbs.

MAKES 3 CUPS

Tender, Mild Herbs

Basil

Chervil

Parsley

Mint

Cilantro

Blanch the herbs (including their stems) in boiling water for 15 seconds. Quickly refresh them under cold running water. Drain and dry them well.

Measure the herbs and place in a blender. Add an equal amount of extra virgin olive oil.

Blend to a smooth paste. Remove to a clean bottle or jar and add 3 times as much olive oil as paste. Shake to combine thoroughly. Store for 1 day. When the herbs have settled, filter the oil through a paper coffee filter. The oil is ready to use.

Store, tightly covered, in the refrigerator for up to 1 week.

Stronger Herbs

Thyme

Rosemary

Marjoram

Oregano

Separate the leaves from the stems; discard the stems. Mince the herbs by hand or in a small ("mini") food processor.

Mix 1 cup minced herb with 2 cups canola oil in a clean jar. Shake well. Let the oil sit at room temperature for 2 hours.

Store, tightly covered, in the refrigerator for up to 1 month.

FRUIT OILS

The clear, strong flavors of these fruits make delectable oils.

MAKES ABOUT 1/2 CUP

Cranberry

Orange

Pineapple

Pomegranate

Pink Grapefruit

Make 2 cups of juice from any of the fresh fruits above (commercially prepared cranberry, orange, and pineapple juices are perfectly acceptable too). Add 1 tablespoon fresh lemon juice to orange or pineapple juice to balance the acidity.

In a nonreactive saucepan, reduce the juice over medium-high heat to a syrup, no more than 1/4 cup. Add an equal amount of the appropriate oil:

Cranberry	Clear Orange Oil
Orange	Basil Oil
Pineapple	Cilantro Oil
Pink Grapefruit	Tarragon Oil
Pomegranate	Ginger Oil

This will make a "broken" sauce, one that separates on the plate. For a somewhat more homogenized sauce, you can whisk very vigorously just before serving.

Store, tightly covered, in the refrigerator up to 2 weeks.

MISCELLANEOUS OILS

The remaining oils are easy, but not easily categorized. Each follows its own method, and several should be prepared a little in advance.

Lobster Oil	Carrot-Cinnamon Oil
Shrimp Oil	Bell Pepper Oil
Peanut Oil	Beet-Ginger Oil
Truffle Oil	Clear Orange Oil
Chive Oil	Dill Oil
Tomato Oil	Watercress Oil

LOBSTER OIL

MAKES 2 1/2 TO 3 CUPS

2 pounds lobster shells, including the heads[*]

1/2 cup canola oil

1 medium carrot, peeled and diced

1 medium onion, peeled and diced

1 stalk celery, peeled and diced

1 clove garlic, peeled and chopped

(continues)

1 bunch tarragon

1 bay leaf

1 bunch parsley, chopped

1/2 bottle dry white wine

4 cups canola oil

Crush the lobster shells (a heavy rolling pin is excellent for this).

In a large, high-sided pot, heat 1/2 cup canola oil until very hot. Carefully add the crushed lobster shells and stir well. Cook over high heat, stirring constantly, for 15 minutes.

Stir in the vegetables and herbs thoroughly. Add the wine. Continue cooking, stirring occasionally, for 15 minutes longer. Add the remaining 4 cups oil and reduce the heat to medium. Cook, stirring occasionally, for 1/2 hour.

Take the pot off the heat. When the mixture is no longer steaming, cover and let it sit at room temperature overnight. It is important to leave the mixture in the pot, as this will intensify the flavor. Do not refrigerate!

Strain the oil through a paper coffee filter into a clean container. Store, tightly covered, in the refrigerator up to 1 month.

Lobster shells can be obtained at most fish markets. If you can get only cooked (bright red-orange) shells, that is fine, but try to get uncooked shells. If cooked shells are used, they should be cooked only 10 minutes in the oil.

SHRIMP OIL

Garnish the oil on a serving plate with some diced tomato and parsley for a very striking presentation.

MAKES ABOUT 4 CUPS

1 pound shrimp shells*

1/2 cup canola oil

1 medium carrot, peeled and diced

1 medium onion, peeled and diced

1 stalk celery, peeled and diced

1 bunch thyme

1 bunch tarragon

1 bay leaf

1 bunch parsley, chopped

1/2 bottle dry white wine

6 cups canola oil

Crush the shrimp shells (a heavy rolling pin is excellent for this).

In a large, high-sided pot, heat 1/2 cup canola oil until very hot. Carefully add the shrimp shells and stir well. Cook over high heat, stirring constantly, for 15 minutes.

Stir in the vegetables and herbs thoroughly. Add the wine. Continue cooking, stirring occasionally, for 15 minutes longer. Add the remaining 6 cups oil and reduce the heat to medium. Cook, stirring occasionally, for 1/2 hour.

Take the pot off the heat. When the mixture is no longer steaming, cover and let it sit at room temperature overnight. It is important to leave the mixture in the pot, as this will intensify the flavor. Do not refrigerate!

Strain the oil through a coffee filter into a clean container. Store, tightly covered, in the refrigerator for up to 1 month.

Shrimp shells can be obtained at most fish markets. Try to find uncooked shells; if only cooked shells are available, cook them in oil only 10 minutes. The color of this oil will not be as bright orange as that of Lobster Oil, but the flavor is very pronounced and rich. Shrimp Oil is an excellent substitution in recipes calling for Lobster Oil.

PEANUT OIL

MAKES ABOUT 6 CUPS

1 pound raw skinless peanuts*
Two 17-ounce bottles canola oil

Roast the peanuts in a 250°F oven until pale gold or amber in color. Let them cool slightly, then process to a paste in a food processor or blender. Combine the paste and oil. Shake well to combine, then strain through a paper coffee filter into a clean container. Store, tightly covered, at room temperature for up to 2 weeks. Do not refrigerate.

*If raw peanuts are not available, use unsalted, roasted peanuts and omit roasting.

TRUFFLE OIL

MAKES 1 1/2 CUPS

2 medium truffles (fresh or canned)
1/4 cup truffle juice (from canned truffles) or port wine
1 cup canola oil

Put the truffles and truffle juice in a blender. Blend to a smooth purée. Add the oil. Blend until smooth and emulsified. Do not strain. Store, tightly covered, in the refrigerator for up to 2 weeks.

CHIVE OIL

The one difficulty with this recipe is obtaining enough chives. If you have less than 3 ounces, use what you have. Measure the juice and add 1 1/2 times as much olive oil.

MAKES 1 1/4 CUPS

2 large bunches chives (3 ounces)
3/4 cup extra virgin olive oil

Rinse the chives in water. Do not pat them dry; the excess water that clings to them will increase the juice.

Put the chives through a juice extractor. You should have 1/2 cup of juice.

Put the chive juice in a food processor or blender. Add the olive oil. Process until thoroughly blended. Store, tightly covered, in the refrigerator until slightly less liquid (about 1 hour). Chive Oil will keep as long as 4 days.

TOMATO OIL

MAKES 3/4 CUPS

4 large beefsteak or plum tomatoes
1/4 cup extra virgin olive oil
1 tablespoon chopped thyme*

Put the tomatoes, unpeeled, through a juice extractor. You should have 3 cups of juice. In a saucepan over medium-high heat, reduce the tomato juice by two-thirds to about 1 cup. Strain through a fine mesh strainer into a clean saucepan. Reduce to a syrup, no more than 1/2 cup. Stir in the olive oil and thyme. Store, tightly covered, in the refrigerator for up to 2 weeks.

Instead of thyme, try minced fresh basil.

CARROT-CINNAMON OIL

MAKES ABOUT 3/4 CUP

2 tablespoons ground cinnamon
2 teaspoons water
1 cup canola oil
1 stick cinnamon
10 medium carrots, peeled
About 3 drops sherry vinegar

Mix ground cinnamon with water to a smooth paste. Put the paste in a clean jar. Add the oil and shake to blend well. Add the cinnamon stick. Let sit for about 2 days, until oil and cinnamon separate. Remove the oil on top with a ladle, being careful not to disturb the solids at the bottom too much. Discard the solids. Filter the oil—not the solids—through a paper coffee filter.

Put the carrots through a juice extractor. You should have 2 cups of juice. In a small saucepan over medium-high heat, reduce the carrot juice to 1 cup. Strain through a fine mesh strainer into a clean saucepan and reduce to a syrup, no more than 1/2 cup. Stir in 1/4 cup cinnamon oil and mix well. Season with vinegar.

BELL PEPPER OIL

The trick here is to reduce the juice slowly and, when it is a syrup, not to add too much olive oil. The resulting oil will be thick and very sweet. Use peppers all of one color, whether they be yellow, red, or green. Let it come to room temperature before shaking and serving.

MAKES 1/2 CUP

8 or 9 large bell peppers, cored and seeded
1/4 cup extra virgin olive oil

Put the peppers through a juice extractor. You should have 2 cups of juice. In a saucepan over medium-high heat, slowly reduce the pepper juice by three-fourths, to about 1/2 cup. Strain through a fine mesh strainer into a clean saucepan. Reduce to a syrup, no more than 1/4 cup. Stir in the olive oil thoroughly. Store, tightly covered, in the refrigerator up to 2 weeks.

BEET-GINGER OIL

MAKES ABOUT 1/3 CUP

8 medium beets (about 2 pounds)
3 drops sherry vinegar
2 tablespoons Ginger Oil (page 39)

Put the beets through a juice extractor. You should have 2 cups of juice. In a saucepan over medium heat, reduce the beet juice to 1/2 cup. Strain through a fine mesh strainer into a clean saucepan and reduce to a syrup, no more than 1/4 cup. Stir in the vinegar and Ginger Oil. Store, tightly covered, in the refrigerator up to 2 weeks.

CLEAR ORANGE OIL

MAKES 2 CUPS

Grated zest of 3 oranges
2 cups canola oil

Combine the zest and oil thoroughly. Let infuse for 2 days.

Strain the mixture through a paper coffee filter. Store, tightly covered, in the refrigerator up to 6 months.

DILL OIL

Dill gives off more juice in the spring and summer (this seems to be true of many herbs and vegetables), and the yield will vary from bunch to bunch. Simply add the same amount of olive oil as dill juice.

MAKES ABOUT 1 CUP

1 bunch dill
About 1/2 cup extra virgin olive oil

Put the dill through a juice extractor. Measure the dill juice and add an equal amount of oil.

Store, tightly covered, in the refrigerator up to 2 weeks.

WATERCRESS OIL

The proportion here, as in the case of Chive Oil, is 1 1/2 times as much olive oil as juice. If you have less than 1/2 cup watercress juice, adjust the amount of oil to be added.

MAKES 1 1/4 CUPS

2 bunches watercress
3/4 cup extra virgin olive oil

Put the watercress through a juice extractor. You should have 1/2 cup of juice.

Put the watercress juice in a food processor or blender. Add the olive oil and process until thoroughly blended. Store, tightly covered, in the refrigerator up to 2 weeks.

Tuna Tartare with Gaufrette Potatoes

This is my version of the classic steak tartare with pommes frites. This tartare combines the soft texture of the ground tuna with the crispness of the gaufrette potatoes. If you don't have a mandoline, you can cut the potato chips by hand. If really pressed for time, use good-quality chips straight from the bag. When buying the tuna, look for fish that is a deep shade of pink, almost red.

SERVES 4

3/4 pound raw tuna, ground (mince by hand or use a food processor)

1/4 cup extra virgin olive oil

3 tablespoons chopped chives

A few drops Tabasco

Salt and freshly ground pepper to taste

Gaufrette Potatoes (recipe follows)

Salmon roe or flying fish eggs

4 teaspoons Chive Oil (page 43)

garnish   12 chives, cut into 3-inch lengths

Combine all ingredients except Gaufrette Potatoes, roe, Chive Oil, and garnish, and mix thoroughly. Cover tightly and refrigerate.

For each serving, make 3 little towers, layering tuna between 3 gaufrettes. Insert 1 chive stick through each tower.

Scatter the roe around each plate and drizzle with a little Chive Oil.

Gaufrette Potatoes

4 medium Idaho potatoes, peeled and trimmed into large ovals
Canola oil, for frying

Using a mandoline set for "gaufrettes" (waffle pattern), slice the potatoes very thin. (If you do not have a mandoline, potatoes may be thinly sliced by hand.) You will need 36 slices. Rinse potatoes in a bowl of cold water and pat dry with paper toweling.

Heat the oil (1-inch deep) until very hot (350° to 375°F). Fry the potato slices in batches (so they don't overlap) on both sides until golden brown and crisp, 5 to 8 minutes. (Potatoes may be baked in the oven instead of frying. They will be crisper and somewhat drier. After slicing potatoes, place on a nonstick baking sheet and brush with butter. Bake in a 450°F oven until golden brown.) Drain on paper toweling and salt them lightly. Set aside.

Tuna Tartare with Assorted Chips and Oils

This version of tuna tartare makes little "sandwiches" of the tuna between small vegetable chips. The brilliant colors of the oils are breathtaking. Drizzle the oils around the plate. You'll begin to believe you are an artist after you "paint" a plate or two. Serve the dish without knives and forks and let your guests use their hands.

SERVES 4

24 Vegetable Chips, any combination of Celeriac, Beet, and Lotus Root (pages 197, 198)

Tuna Tartare (page 46) without Gaufrettes or garnish

2 teaspoons each red Bell Pepper Oil (page 44), Curry Oil (page 39), and Chive Oil (page 43)

Make 3 types of vegetable chips. This may be done up to 1 day in advance.

Prepare the Tuna Tartare. Shape the mixture into small balls no more than 1/2 inch across.

For each serving, sandwich 3 tuna balls between 2 vegetable chips.

Place 3 sandwiches on each of 4 serving plates. Drizzle a little of each oil around the plates.

Cod in a Horseradish Crust

SERVES 4

6 tablespoons unseasoned breadcrumbs, fresh or commercial	1 tablespoon chopped chervil
2 teaspoons sweet butter	1 tablespoon chopped thyme
2 tablespoons freshly grated or commercially prepared white horseradish	1 cup dry white wine
$1/2$ tablespoon chopped rosemary	Four 6-ounce cod fillets
1 tablespoon chopped tarragon	Salt and freshly ground pepper to taste
	$1/2$ cup Horseradish Oil (page 39)
	$1/4$ cup balsamic vinegar

Heat the oven to 450°F.

Combine the breadcrumbs, butter, horseradish, rosemary, tarragon, chervil, and thyme in the workbowl of a food processor. Add 3 tablespoons of the wine and process to a paste.

Spread the top of each piece of cod with equal amounts of the breadcrumb mixture.

Place fillets in a shallow, broiler-proof pan. Pour the remaining wine around them and bake for 10 minutes.

Remove pan from the oven and place it about 3 inches under a preheated broiler. Season fillets with salt and pepper. Broil until the crust is browned.

Place a fillet on each of 4 warmed serving plates. Drizzle Horseradish Oil around the cod and sprinkle a little balsamic vinegar over all.

Cod Cakes with Orange-Basil Oil

Cod and potatoes make wonderful little cakes. Add the chopped basil or not, as you like.
The mixture should not be too moist. Cod cakes are also delicious
with the simple Mustard Wine Sauce on page 196.

SERVES 4

4 cups water	6 tablespoons extra virgin olive oil
1 cup dry white wine	$2/3$ cup milk
1 bay leaf	2 to 3 tablespoons chopped fresh basil or
2 branches thyme	2 teaspoons dried basil
2 cloves garlic, peeled	Flour
1 pound cod fillets	$1/2$ cup Orange-Basil Oil (page 41)
3 large potatoes (2 $1/2$ to 3 pounds), peeled and quartered	

Heat the oven to 400°F.

Combine the water, wine, bay leaf, thyme, and 1 clove of garlic in a large sauté pan. Bring to a simmer over medium-low heat. Add the fish and poach for 10 minutes.

Remove the fish and gently pat dry.

Cook the potatoes in boiling salted water until tender when pierced with a fork, 15 to 20 minutes. Drain the potatoes and dry them in the oven for 10 minutes. Mash them by hand, using a potato masher or a fork. Add the remaining clove of garlic, minced, 3 tablespoons olive oil, and the milk. Mix until smooth. Combine the fish and the potato mixture and mix thoroughly. Stir in the basil. Shape the mixture into small cakes, about 2 inches in diameter. Cover and refrigerate for 1 hour.

Dust each cake lightly with flour. Heat the remaining 3 tablespoons olive oil and sauté the cakes until golden brown, 2 to 3 minutes per side. Serve with Orange-Basil Oil.

Halibut with Truffle
and Yellow Bell Pepper Oil

The green of the fava beans, the yellow of the pepper oil, and the black of the truffle oil make this a striking dish. While the flavor of Truffle Oil is unique, you can substitute red Bell Pepper Oil for an equally distinctive dish. If you like, substitute lima beans for the fava beans.

SERVES 4

1 cup shelled fava beans	6 tablespoons Truffle Oil (page 43) or red Bell Pepper Oil (page 44)
Four 7-ounce halibut fillets	
3 tablespoons sweet butter	6 tablespoons yellow Bell Pepper Oil (page 44)
Salt and freshly ground pepper to taste	

Cook fava beans in boiling salted water until tender, about 5 minutes. Drain and pat dry. Set aside.

In a sauté pan, cook the halibut fillets in 2 tablespoons butter over medium heat until light brown on both sides, about 2 minutes per side. Remove from pan, season with salt and pepper, and keep warm.

Add the beans and remaining tablespoon butter to the pan. Sauté over medium-high heat until hot. Season with salt and pepper. Place a fillet on each of 4 warmed serving plates. Spoon fava beans over the fish. Drizzle the two oils around the plate and serve.

Red Snapper in Potato Flakes
with Tomato Oil

*It has been fashionable to prepare various foods in a potato crust. I think that while "strong" foods
such as lamb can take a crunchy crust, fish and scallops are overpowered by such a coating.
For a delicate potato crust, give fish a light coating of potato flakes. The idea is to keep moisture
in the fish without overpowering its delicate flavor.*

SERVES 4

3 eggs	1/2 cup extra virgin olive oil
Four 7-ounce red snapper fillets	Salt and freshly ground pepper to taste
1 cup instant potato flakes	1/2 cup Tomato Oil (page 43)

Beat the eggs in a shallow bowl. Dip the red snapper fillets in the beaten egg, then
dredge them lightly in potato flakes. Pat the flakes onto the fish so the fillets are nicely coated.

In a sauté pan, heat the olive oil over medium-high heat. Cook the fillets 1 minute per
side. Season with salt and pepper.

Transfer the fillets to warmed serving plates. Drizzle with Tomato Oil.

Sea Scallops with Garlic and Saffron Oil

This dish boasts the classic combination of saffron and garlic that makes bouillabaisse so special.
For a striking variation, make a purée of cooked beets and beat in a little butter. Fill the scallops
with this mixture and refrigerate, tightly covered, overnight. The scallops will turn bright pink.
Sauté them and serve with a vinaigrette of fresh lemon juice, good olive oil,
and some white, creamy-crumbly goat cheese mixed in.

SERVES 4

10 cloves garlic, peeled	1 tablespoon chopped chives
6 tablespoons extra virgin olive oil	2 tablespoons Clarified Butter (page 196) or extra virgin olive oil
1 1/2 pounds large sea scallops	1/2 cup Saffron Oil (page 39) or Tomato Oil (page 43)
4 medium Idaho potatoes	
2 tablespoons sherry vinegar	

Blanch the garlic in boiling water for 15 seconds; drain and repeat 3 times, changing the water each time. Purée in a small food processor or blender. Add 2 tablespoons olive oil and blend again until smooth.

Cut a small pocket into the side of each scallop and pipe in about 1/2 teaspoon of the garlic purée. Cover tightly and refrigerate until needed.

Peel the potatoes. Cook them whole in boiling salted water until tender when pierced with a fork, 15 to 20 minutes.

Drain and cut into 1/2-inch slices. Mix with the vinegar, chives, and remaining 4 tablespoons olive oil.

If scallops are wet, lightly pat dry. Melt the butter over medium-high heat and sauté the scallops until golden brown on both sides. Serve with the potato salad and a drizzle of Saffron Oil.

Shrimp Salad with Curry Oil

This is another warm-and-cold salad, made that much more special
by the addition of vanilla grains to the Curry Oil.

SERVES 4

6 whole Jerusalem artichokes or 6 globe artichoke bases, quartered	1 small bunch cilantro, chopped
2 tablespoons fresh lemon juice	Salt, freshly ground pepper, and paprika to taste
2- to 3-inch piece vanilla bean	24 large shrimp, peeled and deveined
1/2 cup Curry Oil (page 39)	2 tablespoons sweet butter
2 tablespoons extra virgin olive oil	2 cups mixed salad greens

Peel the Jerusalem artichokes and slice very thin. Place them in a bowl of cold water and 1 tablespoon lemon juice until ready to cook.

Split the vanilla bean in half lengthwise and scrape the soft grains into a small bowl (reserve the bean for another use). Add the Curry Oil to the vanilla grains and mix well. Set aside.

Whisk together the olive oil, the remaining 1 tablespoon lemon juice, and the chopped cilantro. Season with salt and pepper and set aside.

Steam the shrimp as directed on page 94 until they are pink throughout, 3 to 4 minutes. Season with salt and paprika.

Drain the artichoke slices. In a medium sauté pan, melt the butter and sauté the artichokes until tender. Season with salt and pepper.

Arrange the salad greens in the center of a large plate. Place the sautéed artichokes around the greens. Toss the cooked shrimp in the cilantro vinaigrette and arrange them on the greens. Spoon vinaigrette over all the shrimp and drizzle a little Curry Oil over all.

Shrimp Skewers with Oysters and Horseradish Oil

*Usually, a seafood mousse is baked. Here, shrimp mousse becomes a
crisp-fried coating for large, succulent shrimp.*

SERVES 4

12 medium shrimp, peeled and deveined	1 cup unseasoned breadcrumbs, fresh or commercial
1 egg white	1 cup extra virgin olive oil
1 cup heavy cream	8 oysters, with their liquor
Salt and cayenne pepper to taste	1/2 cup Horseradish Oil (page 39)
24 large shrimp, peeled and deveined	

Combine the medium shrimp, egg white, cream, salt, and cayenne pepper in a food processor or blender. Process until smooth. Refrigerate mousse until ready to use.

Thread 3 large shrimp on each of 8 skewers. Using a pastry bag, pipe mousse over the shrimp to cover. Dip the shrimp in breadcrumbs to coat. Set aside in the refrigerator on plastic wrap for 30 minutes or until ready to use.

In a large sauté pan or Chinese wok, heat about 1/2 inch olive oil to 375°F. Fry the shrimp until golden brown on all sides, about 5 minutes.

Chop the oysters coarsely and mix them and their liquor with the Horseradish Oil.

Serve 2 skewers per person with the oyster-horseradish sauce.

Cold Cucumber Soup
with Dill Oil

A variation on the first cold soup I made in Thailand when sent there by Louis Outhier.
The hot shrimp are exquisite against the backdrop of ice-cold cucumber soup
and the pungency of Dill Oil. A wonderful summer dish.

SERVES 4

2 cucumbers, peeled, seeded, and coarsely chopped	6 tablespoons sour cream
1 cup plain yogurt	12 large shrimp, peeled and deveined
1 tablespoon chopped dill	$1/4$ cup Dill Oil (page 45)
Salt and cayenne pepper to taste	*garnish* 4 sprigs dill

Combine the cucumbers, yogurt, 1 tablespoon dill, salt, and cayenne pepper in a food processor or blender. Process until smooth.

Combine the cucumber mixture with the sour cream in a medium bowl. Set the bowl in a larger bowl that has been filled with ice and stir occasionally until cool, or cover tightly and refrigerate until cold. Don't prepare the shrimp until the soup is cold.

Steam the shrimp for 1 minute until they are pink. Lightly season with salt and cayenne pepper. Pour the soup into chilled bowls and add the hot shrimp. Garnish with Dill Oil and dill sprigs.

Soft-Shell Crabs
with Carrot-Cinnamon Oil

This is one of the rare cases where it's best to season the food before cooking.
The crab shells protect the meat from the drying effect of salt.

SERVES 4

8 medium soft-shell crabs, dressed	1 teaspoon chopped parsley
Salt and cayenne pepper to taste	1 teaspoon chopped tarragon
3 tablespoons sweet butter	1 teaspoon chopped chives
1 teaspoon chopped chervil	1 teaspoon chopped thyme
1 teaspoon chopped cilantro	1 teaspoon chopped marjoram
1 teaspoon chopped dill	1/2 cup Carrot-Cinnamon Oil (page 44)
1 teaspoon chopped sorrel	

Season crabs with salt and pepper. In a large sauté pan, melt the butter over medium-high heat. Add the crabs and sauté 2 minutes per side. Scatter the herbs over the crabs and cook for 2 minutes longer. Serve 2 crabs per person with a drizzle of Carrot-Cinnamon Oil.

Terrine of Pasta and Crabmeat

The trick to this dish (I think of it as one of my "signature dishes") is to line the mold with plastic wrap so the unmolding is foolproof. This trick works beautifully for any terrine that requires unmolding. You can make the broth and stuff the ziti the day before, or even assemble the terrine the night before. The dish may sound complicated, but it really isn't. Take your time and you'll be amazed at the extraordinary result.

SERVES 15

1 pound ziti	2 tablespoons fresh lime juice
1/2 pound crabmeat, picked over for cartilage	1 teaspoon harissa pepper or Chinese chili paste
1 bunch cilantro	1 tablespoon unflavored gelatin
Salt and freshly ground pepper to taste	1/2 cup Lobster Oil (page 41) or Shrimp Oil (page 42)
2 cups Lobster Broth (recipe follows)	
1 stalk lemongrass	

Cook the ziti in boiling salted water until *al dente* (firm, not mushy). Drain immediately and rinse under cold running water. Set aside.

Combine the crabmeat and cilantro in a food processor or blender. Process until finely chopped. Season with salt and pepper.

Fit a pastry bag with a tip that can be inserted into the ziti. Pipe the crabmeat mixture to fill each piece of pasta.

Line a 1 1/2-quart terrine mold with plastic wrap. Fill the mold with the stuffed ziti, layering them lengthwise in the same direction.

Heat the Lobster Broth, lemongrass, lime juice, harissa pepper, salt, and pepper until hot. Sprinkle the gelatin over the broth and stir to dissolve. When the broth has cooled to room temperature, strain it over the stuffed ziti. Cover tightly and refrigerate overnight.

Unmold and slice about 1/2 inch thick. Serve with a drizzle of Lobster Oil. Garnish with cilantro leaves, if you like.

Lobster Broth

Follow the recipe for Lobster Oil (page 41) but add 1 bunch thyme with the herbs and decrease oil to $1/2$ cup. When the wine has nearly evaporated, add 4 cups water (preferably bottled) and cook over medium-high heat for 20 minutes. Strain.

"Spiked" Sweetbreads
with Red Bell Pepper Oil

Here we do something unusual—we sauté and roast the sweetbreads without blanching them first.

Sweetbreads should never be served pink and blanching is the usual way to avoid that.

Here, braising them in a flavorful liquid accomplishes the same thing.

SERVES 4

7 tablespoons extra virgin olive oil	$1/2$ medium onion, peeled and chopped
1 medium red bell pepper, seeded, deribbed and cut into $1/4$-inch-wide strips	$1/4$ medium carrot, peeled and chopped
	1 cup water
Pinch salt	1 branch of thyme
Four 6-ounce sweetbreads	4 bunches broccoli rabe
3 tablespoons sweet butter	Salt and freshly ground pepper to taste
1 clove garlic, peeled and chopped	$1/2$ cup red Bell Pepper Oil (page 44)

Heat the oven to 550°F.

Heat 2 tablespoons olive oil over medium-high heat. Add the red pepper with a pinch of salt and sauté for 1 minute. "Spike" each sweetbread with 4 or 5 red pepper strips, threading them in one side of the sweetbread, through the center and out the other side.

Heat 3 tablespoons olive oil and the butter over medium-high heat. Add the sweetbreads and sauté until brown on both sides, about 5 minutes. Remove the sweetbreads to an oven-proof dish and scatter with the garlic, onion, and carrot. Put in the oven and roast for 10 minutes. Add water and thyme and cook for 10 minutes longer.

Cook the broccoli rabe in boiling salted water for 5 minutes. Drain thoroughly and sauté in the remaining olive oil until hot.

Drain the sweetbreads, season with salt and pepper, and slice $1/2$ inch thick. Serve with broccoli rabe and a drizzle of red Bell Pepper Oil.

Rabbit Sausage
with Mustard Oil

This incredibly easy preparation makes "sausage" without a machine to stuff forcemeat into casings. Rabbit liver gives the sausage a very distinctive flavor. It should be available from the butcher when you buy the rabbit. You may substitute duck, chicken, or venison for the rabbit; use 1 1/2 pounds of boneless meat. Crimp the foil tightly so water doesn't get in.

SERVES 6

One 3-pound rabbit, boned and cut into 1/4-inch dice	3 ounces foie gras or rabbit or chicken liver, cut into 1/4-inch dice
1 whole chicken breast, skinned, boned and cut into 1/4-inch dice	1/4 cup shelled pistachios, broken into halves, or coarsely chopped, skinned hazelnuts
3 1/2 ounces boiled ham, cut into 1/4-inch dice	Salt and freshly ground pepper to taste
1 egg	1/2 cup Mustard Oil (page 39)

Mix all ingredients except Mustard Oil. Roll in aluminum foil in a long cylinder, about 1 1/2 inches in diameter. Poach in simmering water for 12 minutes. Remove from heat and allow to cool in the water. Slice and serve with a drizzle of Mustard Oil.

Marinated Lemon Chicken
with Fennel Oil

4 whole chicken breasts, halved, skinned, and boned

2 cups fresh lemon juice

2 tablespoons chopped cilantro

1 teaspoon chopped parsley

1 teaspoon chopped chives

1 teaspoon chopped basil

1 teaspoon chopped tarragon

1 teaspoon chopped chervil

2 tablespoons sweet butter

Salt and freshly ground pepper to taste

1/4 cup extra virgin olive oil

1/2 cup Fennel Oil (page 39)

In a deep bowl, combine the chicken, lemon juice, and herbs. Marinate for 10 minutes. Drain chicken, reserving marinade.

In large sauté pan, melt the butter over medium-high heat. Add the chicken and sauté 4 minutes per side. Remove from the pan and season with salt and pepper. Deglaze the pan with 1/4 cup of the marinade. Whisk in the olive oil and bring to a boil. Pour sauce over the chicken. Serve with a drizzle of Fennel Oil.

Grilled Veal with Lobster Béarnaise

This dish is a double tribute to the great cuisiner Escoffier. It brings together Escoffier's concept of mixing meat and shellfish with the master's Béarnaise sauce.

SERVES 4

1 1/2-pound lobster	1/2 cup water
4 slices veal (about 5 ounces each), pounded thin	Pinch salt
1 tablespoon sweet butter	1 cup Lobster Oil (page 41) or Shrimp Oil (page 42)
Salt and freshly ground pepper to taste	1 tablespoon chopped tarragon
2 egg yolks	3 drops fresh lemon juice

Cook lobster in boiling salted water for 2 minutes. Drain and let cool. Remove the meat from the tail and claws. Dice and set aside.

Grill the veal (or sauté in 1 tablespoon sweet butter) until desired doneness. Season with salt and pepper and keep warm.

In a double boiler, whisk together egg yolks and water with a pinch of salt. Cook over boiling water, whisking constantly, until light, fluffy, and slightly thickened. Add the oil in a very thin stream, whisking constantly. Fold in the lobster and tarragon. Add lemon juice and season with salt and pepper. Serve with the veal.

Sautéed Calves' Liver with Beet-Ginger Oil

2 tablespoons sweet butter	Braised Red Cabbage (recipe follows)
Four 7-ounce slices calves' liver	
Salt and freshly ground pepper to taste	*garnish* Beet Chips (page 197)
Potato Purée (recipe follows)	1/2 cup Beet-Ginger Oil (page 44)

Melt the butter over medium-high heat and sauté the liver 1 minute per side. Season with salt and pepper. Serve with Potato Purée and Braised Red Cabbage, and garnish with Beet Chips and Beet-Ginger Oil.

Potato Purée

4 medium purple or Idaho potatoes, peeled and halved
3/4 cup milk, warmed
1 tablespoon sweet butter
Salt

Cook potatoes in boiling salted water until tender when pierced with a fork, 15 to 20 minutes. Beat in the warm milk and butter. Season with salt.

Braised Red Cabbage

2 tablespoons sweet butter
$1/2$ medium onion, thinly sliced
1 pound red cabbage, shredded
Zest of 1 medium orange
$1/2$ cup red wine vinegar
$1/2$ cup red wine
3 tablespoons blueberries
Salt and freshly ground pepper to taste

In a nonreactive pot, melt the butter over medium-high heat; add the onion and cook until translucent. Add the cabbage, orange zest, vinegar, and wine. Cover and cook for 15 minutes. Add the blueberries and cook until cabbage is tender, about 15 minutes longer. Season with salt and pepper.

Venison with Cranberry-Orange Oil

SERVES 4

1 1/2 cups dry red wine	Four 7-ounce venison fillets
3 tablespoons extra virgin olive oil	2 tablespoons sweet butter
2 tablespoons crushed, unsweetened cranberries	1 cup Onion Jam (page 159)
	1/2 cup Cranberry-Orange Oil (page 41)

Combine the wine, 1 tablespoon olive oil, and the cranberries. Marinate the venison in this mixture for 1 day.

Heat the oven to 450°F. In a large sauté pan, melt the butter and 2 tablespoons olive oil over medium-high heat until golden brown. Remove the venison from the marinade; do not pat dry. Sauté 1 1/2 minutes per side, until golden brown. Remove to an oven-proof pan and roast 10 minutes for medium-rare.

Meanwhile, deglaze the sauté pan with the marinade. Reduce to a syrup, no more than 1/4 cup. When the venison is cooked to taste, coat each fillet with the reduced syrup and keep warm.

Put a scant 1/4 cup Onion Jam on each of 4 warmed serving plates. Cut each fillet into 3 slices and arrange over the Onion Jam. Drizzle with Cranberry-Orange Oil.

building block

Vegetable Broths

AN IMPORTANT PART OF MY CUISINE IS THE USE OF VEGETABLE BROTHS. UNLIKE THE BEEF, VEAL, CHICKEN, FISH, AND SHELLFISH STOCKS OF CLASSIC FRENCH CUISINE, WHICH TAKE AS LONG AS 10 HOURS TO prepare, vegetable broths are cooked in 30 minutes.

The broths can be served alone or in combination with flavored and unflavored oils to make uniquely aromatic sauces, perfect accompaniments to fast sautés and steamed dishes; use about $1/2$ cup per serving. Some of my recipes call for the basic broths that follow just as they are, and some work their own variation on the broth theme.

All of the vegetable broths will keep, tightly covered, in the refrigerator for 3 to 4 days. Better yet, freeze them for as long as 1 month.

BASIC VEGETABLE BROTHS

Shallot Broth   **Mushroom Broth**

Mixed Vegetable Broth   **Endive Broth**

Artichoke Broth

Each of these broths has a unique, rich flavor, amazing considering the short cooking time. I have always been fascinated with the Mushroom Broth and its reduction which, after a mere 30 minutes, closely resembles a veal stock and, if reduced further, a veal *demi-glace* that would take a day to prepare.

SHALLOT BROTH

1 tablespoon extra virgin olive oil
1 tablespoon sweet butter
3/4 pound shallots, peeled and thinly sliced (3 cups)
Salt and freshly ground pepper to taste
2 cups water (just enough to cover shallots)

In a pan large enough to hold the shallots in a shallow layer, heat the olive oil and butter over medium-high heat until sizzling. Add the shallots with a pinch of salt and pepper. Sauté over medium-high heat for 10 to 15 minutes, until the shallots are very brown and have caramelized.

Add just enough water to cover the shallots. Stir well, scraping up any browned bits clinging to the pan. Transfer the shallots and broth to a smaller pot.

The water should just cover the shallots; add a little more if necessary.

Boil over medium-high heat for 15 minutes. Strain broth through a fine mesh strainer.

MUSHROOM BROTH

2 tablespoons sweet butter
1 pound white button mushrooms, quartered (about 5 cups)
Salt and freshly ground pepper to taste
2 shallots, peeled and sliced
1 clove garlic, peeled and halved
2 cups water (just enough to cover mushrooms)
2 tablespoons minced parsley

In a pan large enough to hold the mushrooms in a single layer, heat the butter over medium-high heat until sizzling. Add the mushrooms with a pinch of salt and pepper and cook, stirring constantly, until the mushrooms are deep brown and have caramelized, 15 to 20 minutes.

Add the shallots, garlic, and just enough water to cover the mushrooms. Add the parsley and stir well, scraping up any browned bits clinging to the pan. Transfer the vegetables and broth to a smaller pot.

Bring to a boil over medium-high heat and boil for 15 minutes. Strain broth through a fine mesh strainer. The broth will be deep brown in color.

MUSHROOM SYRUP

Mushroom Broth may be reduced over medium-high heat for about 10 minutes longer until just a syrup remains, no more than 1/2 cup. This syrup resembles a veal *demi-glace*. Serve alone as an intensely flavored sauce.

For a sauce with milder flavor, swirl in 2 to 3 tablespoons olive oil or sauce individual servings with 1 tablespoon each Mushroom Syrup and olive oil. Even when the oil is whisked in, the effect on serving will be of a "broken sauce," the gold of the oil and rich brown of the Mushroom Syrup separating slightly—a look I love.

MIXED VEGETABLE BROTH

Mixed Vegetable Broth perfectly complements a sauté of chicken, fish, or shellfish.

4 cups mixed vegetables, coarsely chopped[*]
1 bunch parsley
1/2 cup fresh herbs (any kind)
2 tablespoons extra virgin olive oil (optional)

Put the vegetables, parsley, and other herbs in a medium-size pot and cover with water.

Boil over medium-high heat for 20 minutes. Strain the broth through a fine mesh strainer. Serve alone or swirl in 2 tablespoons olive oil.

Carrots, zucchini, celery, onions, turnips, mushrooms, cabbage, and garlic.

ENDIVE BROTH

3 medium heads endive, thinly sliced (3 cups)
2 tablespoons sweet butter
Salt and freshly ground pepper to taste
2 cups dry white wine
(just enough to cover endives)
2 tablespoons peanut oil (optional)

In a pan large enough to hold endives in a shallow layer, sauté the endives in 2 tablespoons butter with a large pinch of salt and pepper over medium-high heat for 5 minutes. Endives will be soft.

Add just enough wine to cover the endives. Bring to a boil, then reduce the heat to medium-low. Simmer, uncovered, for 15 minutes.

Strain broth through a fine mesh strainer. Serve alone or add 2 tablespoons peanut oil to round out the flavor and make the sauce less acidic.

ARTICHOKE BROTH

4 large or 6 medium artichokes*
Fresh lemon juice
Pinch salt
2 tablespoons extra virgin olive oil
1/2 small onion, peeled and chopped
3 to 4 cups dry white wine (just enough to cover artichokes)
1 teaspoon salt

Trim the hard base from each artichoke. Trim the top down to the fuzzy choke.

Remove all the leaves, trimming until you reach the heart, the rounded base of the artichoke.

Scrape away the choke. Put each trimmed artichoke in water acidulated with a little lemon juice and a pinch of salt (this will prevent discoloration).

In a medium saucepan, heat the olive oil over medium heat. Add the onion and let it sweat in the olive oil for 5 minutes.

Cut each artichoke heart into quarters and add them to the onions.

Add just enough wine to cover the artichokes and the salt. Boil over medium-high heat for 20 minutes. Strain broth through a fine mesh strainer.

If you are pressed for time, the frozen artichoke hearts available in most supermarkets can be used. Simply thaw, quarter, and proceed with the recipe.

Shallot Broth with Flounder

Here is an unstrained variation of the intensely flavored basic Shallot Broth on page 68. While the basic broth is meant to be enjoyed as a sauce, this is a true broth, nearly a soup.

SERVES 4

4 tablespoons sweet butter

1/2 pound shallots, peeled and sliced (2 cups)

Pinch salt

2 cups water

Four 7-ounce flounder fillets

2 tablespoons hazelnut or extra virgin olive oil

1 teaspoon chopped marjoram plus 4 sprigs marjoram, for garnish

Salt and freshly ground pepper to taste

In a large sauté pan, melt the butter over low heat. Add the shallots and a pinch of salt and cook until shallots have caramelized. Add water and simmer for 20 minutes.

Add the fish fillets and poach them for 3 minutes. Gently remove to soup plates. Stir in the hazelnut oil and marjoram; season the broth with salt and pepper. Ladle broth over each serving of fish and garnish with a sprig of marjoram.

Watercress Broth with Yellow Pike

This dish combines two water-loving ingredients: yellow pike and watercress. The intense, peppery flavor of watercress is a delicious foil for the delicate yellow pike. Add the watercress to the fish broth only at the last moment, to preserve its sharp flavor and bright color.

SERVES 4

2 tablespoons sweet butter	2 cups dry white wine
1 medium onion, peeled and thinly sliced	4 cups water
1 leek, washed thoroughly and thinly sliced	1/2 cup sliced button mushrooms
1 stalk celery, chopped	1 bunch watercress, leaves and stems separated
One 3-pound yellow pike or salmon, filleted, head and bones reserved	1 Bouquet Garni (page 196)
	Salt and freshly ground pepper to taste

In a large saucepan, melt the butter over medium-high heat; add the onion, leek, celery, fish bones, and head. Gently cook until vegetables are soft and translucent. (Do not allow them to color.) Add the wine, water, mushrooms, watercress stems, and Bouquet Garni. Simmer for 30 minutes. Strain the broth through a fine mesh strainer into a clean saucepan and keep warm over low heat.

Finely chop the watercress leaves. Cut the fish fillets into 3 × 1/2-inch strips. Heat the broth to a simmer and add the strips of fish. Poach the fish for 1 minute. Gently remove to soup plates. Season the broth with salt and pepper; stir in the chopped watercress. Ladle broth over each serving of fish.

Whiting with Endive Broth

You will be amazed at how beautifully the tangy flavor of endive broth complements mellow whiting, a very delicate, white fish. In the place of my Peanut Oil you can use any commercial peanut oil, so long as it is from a first pressing. To crack peanuts, simply whack them with a heavy pot.

SERVES 4

4 heads endive, 12 leaves reserved and
   remaining leaves chopped
3 tablespoons sweet butter
Pinch sugar
Salt and freshly ground pepper to taste
1 cup dry white wine

2 pounds whiting, cut into 12 pieces
1 tablespoon Peanut Oil (page 43) or
   roasted peanut oil
1 tablespoon cracked black pepper
2 tablespoons cracked raw peanuts

In a pan large enough to hold endives in a shallow layer, sauté the chopped endives over medium heat in 1 tablespoon butter with the sugar, salt, and pepper for 5 minutes. Add the wine and cook until tender, about 15 minutes. Strain the broth through a fine mesh strainer, reserving the cooked endives; set the broth aside.

Combine the cooked endives with about 2 tablespoons broth in a food processor or blender and process until smooth. Set aside.

In a large sauté pan over medium heat, melt 1 tablespoon butter. Add the fillets to the pan. Cook 3 minutes per side. Remove them from the pan, season with salt and pepper, and keep warm.

Sauté the 12 endive leaves in the remaining 1 tablespoon butter until they take on a little color around the edges, about 6 minutes. Heat the endive purée and the remaining broth in separate pans. Whisk the peanut oil into the broth.

Scatter the cracked pepper and peanuts around each of 4 serving plates. Spoon endive purée onto the center of each plate and top with 3 pieces of fish. Place one endive leaf on top of each piece of fish. Spoon some broth around the fish.

Monkfish with Mushroom Syrup

Monkfish has been called "poor man's lobster." To me, it has the flavor and texture of meat.
Monkfish fillets are thick and wide. Cut them in half lengthwise, then cut across. The flesh is soft
enough that, when wrapped in bacon, pieces take on the shape of medallions. This dish always
reminds me of a real "meat and gravy" dish. To complete the presentation, serve this
with a potato purée or Pommes Annette (page 139).

SERVES 4

1 pound monkfish fillets	2 tablespoons chopped parsley
12 slices bacon, double-smoked if possible	Salt and freshly ground pepper to taste
1/4 cup extra virgin olive oil	1/2 cup Mushroom Syrup (page 68)
1 cup shiitake mushrooms, stems discarded and caps washed thoroughly	

Put the monkfish fillets into 12 pieces. Encircle each piece with a slice of bacon and secure these fish medallions with a piece of kitchen string. In a large sauté pan, heat 1 tablespoon olive oil over medium-high heat until hot. Cook the medallions until golden brown on both sides, 5 minutes per side.

In a sauté pan, heat 1 tablespoon olive oil over medium-high heat until hot. Add the mushroom caps and sauté until soft and browned. Sprinkle with parsley and season with salt and pepper.

Warm the Mushroom Syrup and whisk in the remaining 2 tablespoons olive oil. Season with salt and pepper.

Arrange 3 medallions of each on 4 serving plates. Divide the sautéed mushrooms among the plates and spoon sauce around the fish.

Salmon in a Shiitake Shell

Remember to look for large shiitake mushrooms. The salmon and shiitakes have the same texture; the contrast here is in the flavor.

SERVES 4

8 large shiitake mushrooms, stems discarded and caps washed thoroughly	2 eggs
$1^1/2$ pound salmon fillets ($^1/2$ to $^3/4$ inch thick), cut into four 6-ounce pieces, trimmed into round shapes	2 tablespoons sweet butter
	$^1/2$ cup Mushroom Syrup (page 68)
$^1/2$ cup all-purpose flour	2 tablespoons hazelnut or extra virgin olive oil
2 cups unseasoned breadcrumbs, fresh or commercial	2 tablespoons chopped parsley

Steam the mushroom caps over boiling water until soft, 4 to 5 minutes.

Sandwich each piece of salmon between two mushroom caps. Put the flour, breadcrumbs, and the eggs, slightly beaten, in 3 separate bowls. Dip each salmon-mushroom piece first into the egg, then the flour, and finally the breadcrumbs. Repeat the 3 coatings.

Melt the butter in a medium nonstick pan over medium-high heat. When hot, add the salmon-mushroom pieces and cook for 3 minutes per side for medium-rare. Remove from the pan and cover.

Warm the Mushroom Syrup and whisk in the hazelnut oil.

Place 1 salmon-mushroom piece on each of 4 warmed serving plates. Spoon some sauce around the plate and sprinkle with parsley.

Lobster à la Nage

This is one of the simplest and best methods of preparing lobster. Using a relatively small amount of cooking liquid and cooking the lobster in the shell brings out the strongest flavor and a natural sweetness.

SERVES 4

Four 1$^{1}/_{2}$-pound lobsters
$^{3}/_{4}$ cup sweet butter
1 medium carrot, peeled and julienned
1 medium turnip, peeled and julienned
$^{1}/_{2}$ stalk celery
1 medium leek, washed thoroughly and julienned

2 shallots, peeled and finely chopped
Salt and freshly ground pepper to taste
2 cups brut champagne or dry sparkling white wine
2 cups Mixed Vegetable Broth (page 68)
2 tablespoons chopped chervil

Heat the oven to 450°F.

Blanch the lobsters in boiling salted water for 2 minutes. Drain and set aside.

Melt 4 tablespoons butter in a pan. Add the vegetables (except 1 of the shallots), cover and sweat until tender but not soft. Season with salt and pepper. Set aside.

Cut the lobsters in half lengthwise. Separate the claws from the bodies and crack the shells. In a large pot, melt 2 tablespoons butter. Add the remaining shallot, lobsters, vegetables, champagne, and Mixed Vegetable Broth. Cover the pot and cook in the oven for 6 minutes.

Remove the lobster bodies from the pot and continue to cook the claws for 2 minutes longer. Remove claws from the pot.

Place the pot on the stove over high heat and reduce the liquid by half. Whisk in the remaining 6 tablespoons butter. Add the chervil. Serve the lobster, still in the shell if you like, in bowls with some of the broth and vegetables.

Lobster with Parsnip Purée

The essence of any lobster preparation is sweetness and texture. This dish compares the distinctive sweetness and texture of the parsnips, lotus root, and lobster.

SERVES 4

Four 1^1/2-pound lobsters	^{1}/2 cup Mushroom Syrup (page 68)
6 medium parsnips, peeled and diced	^{1}/4 cup Lobster Oil (page 41) or Shrimp Oil (page 42)
4 tablespoons sweet butter	
^{1}/2 cup heavy cream	*garnish* Lotus Root Chips (page 198)
Salt and freshly ground pepper to taste	

Blanch the lobsters in boiling salted water for 2 minutes. Let cool and remove meat from tails and claws.

Cook the parsnips in boiling salted water until tender. Drain and pass through a food mill or ricer. Add 2 tablespoons butter, the cream, and salt and pepper to taste, and keep warm.

Melt the remaining 2 tablespoons butter in a sauté pan over medium heat. Add the lobster meat and sauté on both sides, 3 minutes per side.

While the lobster is cooking, heat the Mushroom Syrup and whisk in the Lobster Oil.

Arrange the lobster on each of 4 warmed serving plates. Add some of the parsnip purée to each plate and garnish with Lotus Root Chips. Spoon some sauce around the lobster.

Shrimp in a Spiced Orange and Sauternes Broth

*This is a wonderful dish for a summer party. Let the guests help themselves
from large serving bowls of shrimp and rice.*

SERVES 4

1 medium carrot, peeled and diced	8 threads saffron
1/2 medium cucumber, peeled, seeded, and diced	1 tablespoon fresh lemon juice
4 medium button mushrooms, diced	32 large shrimp (about 2 pounds), peeled and deveined
1 cup Sauternes or Gewürztraminer	2 tablespoons chopped flat-leaf parsley
1 cup fresh orange juice	Salt and freshly ground pepper to taste
2 tablespoons sweet butter	2 cups Spiced Rice (page 156)
1 tablespoon fresh ginger julienne	

In a large pot, combine the vegetables, Sauternes, orange juice, butter, ginger, saffron, and
lemon juice. Cook for 15 minutes. Add shrimp and cook for 1 minute. Add the parsley and
salt and pepper to taste. Serve in bowls over Spiced Rice.

Cannelloni of Crab with Caramom

6 tablespoons sweet butter	Salt and freshly ground pepper to taste
1 bunch Swiss chard, finely chopped	4 spring roll or egg roll wrappers*
1/2 pound crabmeat, picked over for cartilage	2 cups Mixed Vegetable Broth (page 68)
1/4 cup chopped parsley	1/2 teaspoon cracked green cardamom seed*

Melt 2 tablespoons butter over medium-high heat and add the Swiss chard. Cook until tender, about 4 minutes. In a medium bowl, combine the Swiss chard with the crabmeat and parsley. Season with salt and pepper.

Cook the spring roll wrappers in boiling salted water until soft, about 15 seconds. Drain on paper toweling. Place 1 1/2 to 2 tablespoons of the crabmeat mixture one on each wrapper. Roll the wrappers around the filling into cylinder shapes. Steam over boiling water until heated through, about 5 minutes.

In a small saucepan, boil the Mixed Vegetable Broth with the cracked cardamon seeds until reduced by three-fourths. Whisk in the remaining 4 tablespoons butter and season with salt and pepper. Divide the cannelloni among 4 warmed serving plates and spoon some of the sauce over them.

For an even lighter variation, use rice paper instead of spring roll skins. Soften each 8-inch round of rice paper between layers of damp kitchen toweling for about 5 minutes, until pliable enough to roll without cracking, but not wet. The rounds of rice paper are much larger than spring roll wrappers. Fill them with twice as much crabmeat mixture; roll, then cut in half. Spring roll and egg roll wrappers and rice paper can be found in Asian markets. Cardamom is a very potent spice, so be sure not to overpower the dish. Use green cardamom only, as it is less powerful than the white variety.

Scallops with Artichoke Broth

SERVES 4

1/2 cup shelled fava beans	1 cup Artichoke Broth (page 69)
4 medium artichokes	2 teaspoons chopped savory
4 tablespoons extra virgin olive oil	2 tablespoons sweet butter
Salt and freshly ground pepper to taste	18 ounces scallops
2 tablespoons grated hard goat cheese or Parmesan	

Cook the fava beans in boiling salted water until tender, about 5 minutes. Drain and keep warm.

Trim the hard base from each artichoke. Trim the top down to the fuzzy choke. Remove all the leaves, trimming until you reach the heart, the rounded base of the artichoke. Scrape away the choke. (If you prepare the artichoke hearts in advance, save the trimmings to make Artichoke Broth. Put the trimmed artichokes in water acidulated with a little lemon juice and a pinch of salt to prevent them from discoloring.) Cut the artichokes into fine julienne strips. Heat 2 tablespoons olive oil over medium heat. Add the artichokes and season with salt and pepper. Sauté until hot, about 2 minutes. Remove them to a bowl and stir in the cheese. Set aside.

Reduce the Artichoke Broth by half and whisk in the remaining 2 tablespoons olive oil. Add the savory and the fava beans.

Melt the butter in a medium sauté pan over medium-high heat. Add the scallops and sauté until lightly brown on both sides. Season with salt and pepper. Divide among 4 warmed serving plates. Spoon sauce around the scallops and scatter reserved sautéed artichokes and cheese over all.

Lamb in a Potato Crust

This is one of the favorite dishes at Lafayette. The potato crust does not overpower the strong flavor and texture of the lamb. Be sure to sear the lamb quickly before covering it with the unwashed potato shreds. This searing seals in the juices. A nonstick pan is important for this recipe.

SERVES 4

3/4 cup extra virgin olive oil	1/4 cup Mushroom Syrup (page 68)
2 racks of lamb, the eyes trimmed and cut into eight 4-ounce medallions (have the butcher trim them for you)	1 medium tomato, peeled, seeded, and diced
Salt and freshly ground pepper to taste	4 basil leaves, cut into ribbons, plus 4 sprigs basil for garnish
4 medium Idaho potatoes	

Heat 2 tablespoons olive oil over medium-high heat until very hot. Sear the medallions about 10 seconds per side. Remove immediately from the pan. Season with salt and pepper and set aside.

Peel and shred the potatoes. (Do not put in water.) Lightly season with salt. Pat the shredded potatoes around each lamb medallion, pressing firmly between your hands so the potatoes adhere.

In a large nonstick pan, heat 1/2 cup olive oil over medium-high heat (add more oil if necessary for a depth of 1/2 inch). Add the lamb medallions and reduce heat to medium. Cook until potatoes are brown and crisp on both sides.

In a small saucepan, warm the Mushroom Syrup and whisk in the remaining 2 tablespoons olive oil. Add the tomato and basil. Season with salt and pepper.

Place one medallion on each of 4 warmed serving plates. Pour the sauce around each. Garnish with a sprig of fresh basil.

Lamb with Artichokes and Olives

This dish reminds me of the south of France, where lamb fillets would be served
in a classic Provençal "crust" of artichokes and olives.

SERVES 4

4 medium artichokes

6 tablespoons extra virgin olive oil

1 ounce pitted black olives, chopped

1 cup unseasoned breadcrumbs, fresh or
commercial

2 racks of lamb, the eyes trimmed and
about 1 pound each (have the butcher
trim them for you)

Salt and freshly ground pepper to taste

2 cups Artichoke Broth (page 69)

1 tablespoon fresh thyme leaves

Prepare artichokes as directed on page 79.

Finely dice the artichoke hearts. Sauté in 2 tablespoons olive oil for 1 minute. Combine them in a medium bowl with the olives and breadcrumbs.

Cut the lamb into 1/2-inch-thick medallions. In a large sauté pan, heat 2 tablespoons olive oil over medium-high heat. Add the lamb and sauté until desired doneness, about 1 minute per side. Transfer to a broiler-proof pan large enough to hold them in a single layer. Season with salt and pepper and top with the olive mixture. Put under a preheated broiler until very hot, about 30 seconds. Remove from broiler and keep warm.

In a small saucepan, heat the Artichoke Broth over medium-high heat until boiling. Reduce by half. Whisk in the remaining 2 tablespoons olive oil and add the thyme leaves. Season with salt and pepper and serve with the lamb.

Truffled Lamb
with Fava Bean Purée

This dish, particularly when made with truffles, is a very special preparation

and should be served at a dinner party for dear friends or in honor of a very special occasion.

SERVES 4

2 large, fresh black truffles or 1 1/2 cups dried mushrooms (morels, porcini, black trumpet, or chanterelles)*	3 pounds fava beans, shelled, or 2 cups shelled lima beans
All-purpose flour	2 tablespoons heavy cream
1 egg	2 tablespoons sweet butter
2 racks of lamb, the eyes trimmed and about 1 pound each, cut into four 4-ounce loins (have the butcher trim them for you)	2 cups fresh black trumpet mushrooms, washed
	5 tablespoons hazelnut or extra virgin olive oil
Salt and freshly ground pepper to taste	1/2 cup Mushroom Syrup (page 68)

Finely chop the truffles (if using dried mushrooms, please see note below). Put the flour in a shallow bowl, the egg (lightly beaten) in another, and the chopped truffles in a third. Dip the lamb first into the flour, then the egg, and then the truffles. Season with salt and pepper and set aside.

Cook the beans in boiling salted water until tender, about 1 1/2 minutes. Drain them, then purée in a food processor or blender. Add the cream and 1 tablespoon butter and process until smooth. Season with salt and pepper and keep warm.

In a medium sauté pan, melt 1 tablespoon butter over medium-high heat. Add the fresh trumpet mushrooms and sauté until their liquid has evaporated. Season with salt and pepper and keep warm.

If using dried mushrooms instead of truffles, make sure they are very dry and hard. Grind them in a food processor or blender until coarsely chopped (but not dust). Dip the lamb in egg (omit the flour), then coat with a thin layer of mushrooms. Allow to stand in the refrigerator for 1 hour. (The juices from the meat will slightly hydrate the mushrooms.) Proceed with the recipe.

Heat the oven to 450°F. In a large sauté pan, heat 2 tablespoons oil over medium-high heat until hot. Add the lamb and sear about 10 seconds per side. Remove the lamb to an ovenproof dish, put it in the oven, and roast for approximately 10 minutes (for medium doneness).

Heat the Mushroom Syrup and whisk in the remaining 3 tablespoons oil. Season with salt and pepper and keep warm.

Slice the lamb $1/2$ inch thick and arrange on a serving plate with the bean purée. Pour the mushroom sauce over the lamb and garnish with the mushrooms.

Breast of Pheasant Parmentier

My version of a classic Shepherd's Pie, which combines ground meat with a crust of mashed potatoes. Here the otherwise tough leg of pheasant is ground. You may substitute two 2- to 3-pound baby chickens for the pheasants. Antoine-August Parmentier popularized the potato—virtually single-handedly—in the early nineteenth century. You may be sure that any dish called "Parmentier" features potatoes.

SERVES 4

2 pheasants, breasts and legs removed, breasts skinned and boned	1/2 cup warm milk
1/2 cup dry white wine	1/4 cup hazelnut or extra virgin olive oil
1/2 medium carrot, peeled and diced	Salt and freshly ground pepper to taste
1/2 medium onion, peeled and diced	1 sheet phyllo dough
1/2 stalk celery, diced	5 tablespoons sweet butter
1 Bouquet Garni (page 198)	10 Brussels sprouts, leaves separated
2 medium Idaho potatoes, peeled and quartered	2 cups Mushroom Syrup (page 68)
	2 tablespoons chopped chives

Heat the oven to 550°F.

Braise pheasant legs in oven with wine, carrot, onion, celery, and Bouquet Garni. Cook until meat is tender, about 30 minutes. Grind or finely chop the leg meat and moisten it with the cooking liquid to form a paste. Discard remaining liquid and vegetables. Set the meat mixture aside.

Cook the potatoes in boiling salted water until tender when pierced with a fork, 15 to 20 minutes, and mash by hand, using a potato masher or fork. Add the milk and 2 tablespoons hazelnut oil. Mix to a purée. Season with salt and keep warm.

Cut eight 4-inch rounds from the phyllo. Make 4 stacks of 2 rounds each. Melt 2 tablespoons butter and brush the top rounds lightly. Place on a nonstick baking sheet and bake 3 to 4 minutes, until golden brown. Set aside.

Blanch the Brussels sprouts in boiling salted water until barely wilted, about 30 seconds. Drain and set aside.

In a large sauté pan, melt 3 tablespoons butter over medium-high heat. Add the pheasant breasts and sauté on both sides for 5 minutes in all. Season with salt and pepper.

Warm the Mushroom Syrup and whisk in 2 tablespoons hazelnut oil. Season with salt and pepper.

Divide the meat mixture among each of 4 warmed serving plates, spreading it into a 4-inch circle. Top with a $^1/4$-inch layer of potato purée. Place Brussels sprouts around the outside edge of the potatoes. Top with a round of phyllo. Slice the pheasant breast and place around the plate. Sprinkle with chives and pour some of the sauce over the breast slices.

Simple Sautés and Steamed Dishes

THE VEGETABLE JUICES, VINAIGRETTES, FLAVORED OILS, AND BROTHS PERFECT-
LY DEFINE SIMPLE COOKING FOR ME. THEY TRANSFORM QUICKLY SAUTÉED AND
STEAMED MEAT, POULTRY, FISH, AND SHELLFISH INTO PERFECTLY SEASONED,
luxurious dishes in practically no time.

The sautés and steamed dishes that follow take no longer than 15 minutes to prepare. Nothing could be easier at the end of a hectic day. If you
have made any of the juices, vinaigrettes, flavored oils, or broths ahead of
time, dinner can be on the table in a matter of minutes. You might first try
each sauté or steamed dish with one of the suggested "building blocks," but
improvise as you like and your imagination won't disappoint you.

SAUTÉING

Steak

Red meat (and the thicker fishes such as monkfish, swordfish, halibut, and
salmon) contains muscle fiber that contracts when the meat is sautéed. After
meat is sautéed, it should not be eaten immediately, but allowed to "rest" for
up to 5 minutes. Even the best quality red meat can be tough if eaten immediately after cooking. The resting period allows the fibers to expand again,
making a good steak even more tender. The meat will continue to cook after
it has been removed from the pan.

Remember:

- When buying a steak, whether in the supermarket or from your butcher, look for a well-marbled cut. A marbled appearance is caused by streaks of white fat throughout the beef; these streaks of fat make beef more tender. A piece of red meat without marbling, no matter how fresh, will be tough. Only dark red beef is fresh. If the color is anything but dark red, pass it by.

- Never season meat before cooking! Salt and pepper will draw out the juices, leaving it dry. Season immediately after cooking, and the seasonings will be absorbed by the meat while it rests.

- When meat is quickly seared on all sides, a crust is formed that seals in juices and flavor. This makes for the best sautés. The cooking time in the sauté methods is brief, and the food finishes cooking during the resting time.

- Allow meat to rest for 5 minutes covered with aluminum foil or a plate.

Step 1: In a sauté pan, cook 1 tablespoon of sweet butter and 1 tablespoon of olive or vegetable oil over medium-high heat until golden brown.

Step 2: Place a 1-inch-thick steak in the pan. Do not season.

Step 3: For medium-rare meat, cook 3 to 4 minutes per side.

Step 4: Remove the steak from the pan and immediately season to taste with salt and freshly ground pepper. Cover with aluminum foil or a plate and let rest for 5 minutes.

Serve with *Broccoli juice, Basil Vinaigrette (page 16), Paprika Oil (page 39), Mushroom Broth (page 68), or Mushroom Syrup (page 68) mixed with an equal amount of extra virgin olive oil.*

Veal Scallopini

Veal, the meat of a young calf, should not be red like mature beef. When purchasing veal, look for as light a pink as you can find. If the color is anything but pale pink (sometimes called "white"), the veal is too old and will not be tender.

I find the scallopini available precut in supermarkets a little too thin. Have your butcher cut the veal no thinner than 1/4 inch thick.

Step 1: In a sauté pan, cook 1 tablespoon of sweet butter and 1 tablespoon of olive oil or vegetable oil over medium-high heat until golden brown.

Step 2: Place the veal in the pan. Do not season.

Step 3: For pink veal, cook about 1 minute per side if 1/4 inch thick; 2 minutes per side if 1/2 inch thick. If you want the veal less pink, cook 15 to 30 seconds longer per side.

Step 4: Remove the veal from the pan and immediately season to taste with salt and freshly ground pepper. Cover with aluminum foil or a plate and let rest for 3 minutes.

Serve with   *Citrus Vinaigrette (page 17), Curry Vinaigrette (page 17), Horseradish Oil (page 39), any of the Bell Pepper Oils (page 44), Mushroom Broth (page 68), Mushroom Syrup (page 68), or Artichoke Broth (page 69).*

Chicken Breast

A boneless breast of chicken is less fibrous than beef. It does not need as long a resting time after cooking. In order to seal in the juices, cook the chicken breast over medium-high heat for 2 minutes on one side, then reduce the heat to medium-low and cook for 8 to 10 minutes on the other side. The chicken will be thoroughly cooked but still moist. One way to tell whether a chicken breast is cooked is to lift the little flap of meat (the *suprême*) on the underside. If it lifts easily, the meat should be done.

Step 1: In a sauté pan, cook 1 tablespoon of sweet butter and 1 tablespoon of olive or vegetable oil over medium-high heat until golden brown.

Step 2: Place a skinless, boneless half chicken breast in the pan, thick side down. Do not season.

Step 3: Cook for 2 minutes over medium-high heat. Turn the chicken breast over, reduce the heat to medium-low and cook for 8 to 10 minutes longer, depending upon thickness.

Step 4: Remove the chicken breast from the pan and immediately season with salt and freshly ground pepper. Cover with aluminum foil or a plate and let rest for 3 to 5 minutes.

Serve with   *Pineapple juice, Soy and Ginger Vinaigrette (page 16), Curry Oil (page 39), and red Bell Pepper Oil (page 44), or Artichoke Broth (page 69).*

Pork Chop

Pork has a rich, satisfying flavor. Trim the meat from the bone and trim away any visible fat.

Step 1: In a sauté pan, cook 1 tablespoon of sweet butter and 1 tablespoon of olive or vegetable oil over medium-high heat until golden brown.

Step 2: Place a 1-inch-thick pork chop in the pan. Do not season.

Step 3: Cook for 2 minutes over medium-high heat. Turn the pork chop over, reduce the heat to medium-low, and cook for 7 minutes longer.

Step 4: Remove the pork from the pan and immediately season with salt and freshly ground pepper. Cover with aluminum foil or a plate and let rest for 5 minutes.

Serve with *Juniper Vinaigrette (page 18), Peanut Vinaigrette (page 18), Cumin Oil (page 39), Ginger Oil (page 39), Mustard Oil (page 39), Mushroom Broth (page 68), or Mushroom Syrup (page 68).*

Fish

In France, a young chef is taught to examine fresh fish scrupulously, both at the market and when it arrives at the restaurant. In New York, I try to visit the Fulton Fish Market at least once every two weeks, early in the day (3:00 or 4:00 A.M.), to examine the fish and shellfish purchased by my supplier.

Fish is never fresher than when it is whole. In purchasing whole fish, look for these signs:

- A fish stall and its produce should have a briny, fresh smell. Fish that has a pronounced "fishy" odor has been out of the sea too long.
- The eyes of the fish should be bright, clear, and bulging, not cloudy or sunken. If the eyes are concave, rather than rounded, the fish is not fresh.
- The gills should be bright red, never brownish.

- The flesh of the fish should be firm, not soft or mushy.

If you are buying fillets, try to purchase them directly from a fishmonger, avoiding prepackaged fish whenever possible. Again, fillets—even prepackaged—should not have a strong odor and should be firm to the touch.

To sauté fish properly, you must be careful not to dry it out. In my early days at L'Auberge de I'lll, I was taught that coating the fish before sautéing will not only give it wonderful flavor but ensure that it stays moist.

Bear in mind for both thin fish (flounder, sole, red snapper, salmon fillet, and black bass) and thick fish (halibut, monkfish, salmon, and swordfish steaks):

- Never season the fish before cooking. Seasoning will draw the juices out during cooking and the result will be tough, chewy fish.
- For thin fish, use one of the four methods on page 90 to make a crust to seal in moisture and flavor. Season immediately after cooking. Let the fish rest, covered, for 1 to 2 minutes.
- For thick fish, no crust is necessary as the fish is thick enough to retain moisture. Season immediately after cooking. Let the fish rest, covered, for 3 minutes.
- When fish is perfectly cooked, it is translucent on the inside and moist

throughout. Doneness is really a matter of taste. Americans have been taught to cook fish until it flakes. To me, that means the fish is slightly overcooked. Prepare the fish to suit yourself.

Thin Fish (Flounder, Sole, Black Bass, Red Snapper, Salmon Fillet)

Both Escoffier and Alibab, two of the greatest lions of French cooking, teach that a simple coating protects delicate fish against moisture loss. I like four simple methods of coating fish.

- A flour coating (a technique known as *meunière*, after the French word for miller).
- An egg wash.
- Potato flakes. Instant potato flakes, believe it or not, provide an interesting foil for the delicate nature of fish.
- The skin of the fish, left on one side of the fillet. Ask your fishmonger to fillet the fish this way for you.

Meunière

Step 1: Dip 1 large or 2 medium fillets in all-purpose flour. Gently shake off any excess so only a thin coating remains.

Step 2: In a sauté pan, cook 1 tablespoon of sweet butter and 1 tablespoon of extra virgin olive oil over medium-high heat until golden brown.

Step 3: Place the fish in the pan (do not season) and sauté for the following times:

> *Sole*: 1 minute 15 seconds per side.
> *Salmon Fillet, Flounder, Black Bass, Red Snapper*: 1 minute per side.

If the fillet is very thin, less than $1/4$ inch, the cooking time will be a few seconds less than indicated. If the fish is thicker, cook a few seconds longer.

Step 4: Remove the fish from the pan and immediately season to taste with salt and freshly ground pepper.

Step 5: Let the fish rest for 1 to 2 minutes (for salmon, 2 to 3 minutes). It isn't necessary to cover the fish.

Egg Wash and Potato Flakes

Step 1: In a sauté pan, cook 1 tablespoon of sweet butter and 1 tablespoon of extra virgin olive oil over medium-high heat until golden brown.

Step 2: *Egg Wash:* Beat 1 egg and 1 tablespoon of water with a whisk or fork. Dip 1 large or 2 medium fillets in the egg. Let any excess egg drip off so only a thin coating remains.

Potato Flakes: Coat each fillet with a thin layer of potato flakes. Press the flakes into the flesh of the fish. Gently shake off any excess so only a thin coating remains.

Step 3: Place the fish in the pan (do not season) and sauté for the times given above.

Step 4: Let the fish rest for 1 to 2 minutes (for salmon, 2 to 3 minutes). It isn't necessary to cover the fish.

Skin

Leaving the skin on one side of a fillet provides the most natural protection against loss of moisture, and adds the luxurious flavor of the sea.

Step 1: Sauté the fish, skin side first, in sweet butter and oil as for meunière. Remove from pan.

Step 2: Season and let rest for the recommended times.

Thick Fish (Halibut, Salmon and Swordfish Steaks, Monkfish)

Step 1: In a sauté pan, cook 1 tablespoon of sweet butter and 1 tablespoon of extra virgin olive oil over medium-high heat until golden brown.

Step 2: Reduce the heat to medium. Place the fish (1 inch thick) in the pan and cook 3 to 4 minutes per side. (Monkfish, being the thickest, will need a full 4 minutes per side.)

Step 3: Remove the fish from the pan and immediately season with salt and freshly ground pepper. Cover with aluminum foil or a plate and let rest for 3 minutes.

The fish sautés marry perfectly with many of the vegetable juices, vinaigrettes, flavored oils and—especially—the broths.

Try fish with asparagus or fennel juice, Citrus Vinaigrette (page 17), Orange-Basil Oil (page 41), Shallot Broth (page 68), or Endive Broth (page 69).

Shellfish

Lobster, shrimp, and scallops are favorites both in France and the United States. There are some simple rules to follow:

Lobster: While most people seem to want lobster in the spring and, especially, summer, lobsters taste their best in late fall and early winter—October, November, and December—after the lobster moults in the summer or early fall.

Buy only live lobsters. Wrap the lobster loosely in wet newspaper to keep it moist.

One-and-a-half-pound lobsters, about 5 to 6 years old, are ideal. They are large enough to be sweet, but not so old as to be tough. Occasionally a very large lobster will be sweet and tender, but you cannot count on it.

Female lobsters are more tender than males and their roe enhances flavor. You can tell the sex of a lobster: In the male, the first little appendages at the base of the tail (toward the head) are hard, while those of the female are rather soft.

Scallops: In France, fresh scallops can be purchased at the market in their shells, with the rosy orange coral still attached. Scallops in the shell are virtually impossible to find in the United States. That is a pity, because the roe is delicious. When buying scallops, make sure they are firm, translucent, and, above all, sweet-smelling.

Shrimp: Shrimp should not smell "fishy" if they are fresh. Fresh, uncooked shrimp, in the shell or peeled, should be light gray. If the shrimp are blackened, or if they are soft, they are not fresh enough.

For a quick sauté, sea scallops and shrimp are perfect, the fastest of all sautés. When sautéed, shellfish requires no resting time.

Shrimp (*3/4 pound medium shrimp serves 2*)

Shrimp may be sautéed peeled or in the shell. If sautéing medium shrimp in the shell, add 30 seconds to the cooking time.

Step 1: In a sauté pan, cook 1 tablespoon of sweet butter and 1 tablespoon of extra virgin olive oil over medium-high heat until golden brown.

Step 2: Place the shrimp in the pan. Sauté over medium-high heat 45 to 60 seconds per side (1 1/2 minutes per side for large shrimp, 2 minutes per side for jumbo).

Step 3: Remove the shrimp from the pan and immediately season with salt and freshly ground pepper.

Serve with *Carrot, zucchini, leek, broccoli, or asparagus juices, any of the herb vinaigrettes, Curry Vinaigrette (page 17), Lobster or Shrimp Vinaigrette (page 19), Ginger Oil (page 41), Curry Oil (page 41), or any of the broths (try Lemongrass Broth, page 130).*

You can also merely add a little extra virgin olive oil, thyme, and minced garlic to the pan after the shrimp have been removed. Heat for 30 seconds and pour over the shrimp.

Sea Scallops (*3/4 pound serves 2*)

Cut the scallops so that they are approximately (but no thinner than) 1/2 inch thick. Some sea scallops are smaller than others and may be left whole. Lightly pat dry.

Step 1: In a sauté pan, cook 1 tablespoon sweet butter and 1 tablespoon extra virgin olive oil over medium-high heat until golden brown.

Step 2: Lightly coat the scallops with all-purpose flour (meunière) or leave them plain.

Step 3: Place the scallops in the pan. Do not season. Sauté 30 seconds per side.

Step 4: Remove the scallops from the pan and immediately season with salt and freshly ground pepper.

My favorite seasoning is just a little minced fresh garlic and some fresh thyme cooked in the butter and oil after the scallops are removed from the pan.

Serve with   *A vegetable juice, such as Zucchini Juice Sauce with Thyme (page 1), any herb vinaigrette or herb oil, or any of the broths. Finally, try the Mustard Wine Sauce (page 196).*

STEAMING

Steaming is a perfect way to simply cook poultry, fish, and shellfish. It cooks rapidly without robbing the food of its juices. In the restaurant kitchen I use a traditional Chinese bamboo basket steamer. You can use any form of steamer, whether purchased or improvised.

Cooking with steam means rapid cooking with intense heat. I have devised a method of protecting the fish or whatever I want to steam by wrapping it in plastic wrap before placing it in the steamer. This prevents direct contact with steam and creates a gentle "second steaming" within the plastic. The wrapping saves all the cooking juices. I use a plastic wrap formulated for use in microwave ovens—it is specially made to withstand high temperatures. Shrimp does very well with or without the protection of plastic wrap. As you see from the chart of steaming times that follows, shrimp cook more quickly without the plastic.

Steaming works best when the food to be cooked—shrimp, fish steaks, whatever—is arranged in a single layer. Don't stack scallops, for example; instead, arrange them in a flat package. You may scatter a small quantity of half-cooked cut-up vegetables over the food in the package. The vegetables will finish cooking at the same time.

Steaming in Plastic Wrap

Step 1: Tear off a square of plastic wrap large enough to hold the food in a flat package. Place the food on the plastic.

Step 2: Flavor the food with a scattering of fresh herbs and 1 tablespoon of sweet butter or extra virgin olive oil. Do not season with salt and pepper as this will draw moisture from the food.

Step 3: Wrap the contents securely into a flat package. Place the package in a steamer set over rapidly boiling water and cover.

Step 4: Steam for the time given in the recipe, or use the guide that follows.

Step 5: Carefully unwrap the package. (Scissors or a sharp knife will make opening the hot package easier.)

Step 6: Season immediately after steaming.

Serve with *Any of the juices, vinaigrettes, lavored oils, or broths.*

Thick Fish (1 inch thick)	
Halibut	7 minutes
Monkfish, Swordfish, and Salmon Steaks	10 minutes
Sea Scallops	7 to 8 minutes
Shrimp	
Medium	5 to 7 minutes
Large	8 minutes
Jumbo	10 minutes
Boneless Half Chicken Breast	15 minutes

Steaming without Plastic Wrap (Shrimp only)

Step 1: Arrange 6 large shrimp in a single layer in a steamer over rapidly boiling water and cover.

Step 2: Steam for 1^1/$_2$ minutes.

Step 3: Remove shrimp from the steamer and let rest 30 seconds. For shrimp more well done, cover before the resting period.

Phyllo

PHYLLO DOUGH IS AN AMAZING ALTERNATIVE TO THE FLAKY PUFF PASTRY, PATE FEUILLETÉE, THAT IS A STAPLE OF FRENCH CUISINE. PATE FEUILLETÉE IS SOMEWHAT COMPLICATED TO MAKE, COMBINING A pastry base with large quantities of butter, and it takes about six hours to prepare.

Phyllo dough is made from only flour and water. It is light and very crisp. Though you won't want to make it at home, it is inexpensive, easy to find, and ready to use immediately. It can be purchased in most supermarkets and specialty shops and comes tightly wrapped with about 20 sheets of dough per box.

The phyllo dough recipes that follow can be completed in less than 30 minutes. It is important to remember that, once unwrapped, phyllo dough dries out quickly. Always cover phyllo with a damp kitchen towel when not working with it, and rewrap any unused dough tightly and store it in the refrigerator.

Phyllo is very delicate, but easily mended. Don't worry if it tears while you are working with it. Just match the torn edges, press them together and proceed with the recipe.

You can make these recipes, up to a point, ahead of time. Prepare any fillings and the like in advance, but assemble the dish at the last minute. This will ensure that the phyllo is perfectly crisp.

I use phyllo dough in various ways:

- To wrap foods in the fashion of Beef Wellington or in little packages or "purses."
- To make strudel-like dishes.
- To make triangular appetizers (I think of them as "bricks"), side dishes, and tarts.

HOW TO WORK WITH PHYLLO DOUGH

Unwrap only the number of sheets of dough called for in the recipe. (Make sure frozen dough has thawed entirely before separating sheets. If they are still partially frozen, they will be very brittle.) Trim to the desired shape and size. Keep phyllo not in use covered with plastic wrap or a damp kitchen towel while completing the recipe. Tightly rewrap extra dough and store it in the refrigerator.

Bake unfilled phyllo dough in a 400° to 450°F oven, as called for in the recipe, and adjust the oven rack to the lowest position. You need not grease a pan for any of the phyllo dough recipes, but a nonstick baking sheet is useful.

Salmon Leaves
with Rosemary Oil

This dish combines the soft texture of salmon with the crunch of phyllo.

It is a perfect summer appetizer.

SERVES 4

8 sheets phyllo dough, cut into 10-inch rounds	1 pound boneless salmon fillet, very thinly sliced
1/3 cup Rosemary Oil (page 41)	Salt and freshly ground pepper to taste
8 sprigs fresh rosemary	

Heat the oven to 450°F. Adjust the oven rack to the lowest position.

Brush one round of phyllo lightly with Rosemary Oil. Sprinkle with leaves from one sprig of rosemary. Cover with a second round of phyllo and press down lightly. Repeat with the remaining rounds of phyllo. Place the rounds, not overlapping, on nonstick baking sheets. Bake until golden brown, about 5 minutes.

Cover four 10-inch oven-proof plates with layers of sliced salmon. Brush with Rosemary Oil. Set under a preheated broiler, 6 to 8 inches from the heat, and cook for 1 minute. Season with salt and pepper. Place one phyllo round on top of each plate and garnish with a sprig of rosemary.

Alsatian Tart

This is a lighter version of a traditional Alsatian dish I grew up with. I have looked for—but never found—an American substitute for fromage blanc, the white cheese my mother made every day from raw milk. The following method for fromage blanc is simple, inexpensive, and works beautifully.

MAKES 1 TART

4 sheets phyllo dough, cut into 10-inch rounds

2 tablespoons sweet butter plus 2 teaspoons melted butter

$1/2$ cup sliced onion

3 slices bacon, cut across into very thin slices

$1/4$ of 1 egg yolk

$1/2$ cup Fromage Blanc (recipe follows)

2 tablespoons sour cream

Salt and freshly ground pepper to taste

Heat the oven to 400°F. Adjust the oven rack to the lowest position.

Stack the phyllo rounds and brush the top round with melted butter. Place on a nonstick baking sheet and bake for 5 minutes. Turn over and bake for 3 minutes longer. Set aside.

In a medium sauté pan, melt the butter over medium-high heat. Add onion and sauté until caramelized. Remove onion and set aside. Add the bacon to the pan and cook until crisp. Drain and set aside.

Mix together the egg yolk, Fromage Blanc, sour cream, salt, and pepper. Spread evenly over the phyllo. Sprinkle with bacon and onion. Bake for 10 minutes.

Fromage Blanc

MAKES 1 $^1/_2$ TO 2 CUPS

4 cups milk
2 tablespoons fresh lemon juice
Cheesecloth

Bring the milk to a rolling boil, then take it off the heat.

Stir in the lemon juice. The milk will immediately curdle, separating into whey and white *fromage blanc*[*]. Cover the pot and leave it at room temperature for 2 hours or until cool.

Strain through a double thickness of cheese cloth, pressing out all the liquid.

[*]*Store fromage blanc, tightly covered, in the refrigerator up to one week.*

Shrimp, Tomato, and Cilantro Tart

This dish also works well with fresh sea scallops or crab.
Use about $1/2$ pound of either instead of the shrimp.

MAKES 1 TART

4 sheets phyllo dough, cut into 10-inch
  rounds
2 tablespoons Lobster Oil (page 41) or
  Shrimp Oil (page 42)
1 cup sliced scallions

8 large shrimp, peeled and deveined
2 tablespoons peeled, seeded, and diced
  tomato
$1/4$ teaspoon chopped fresh ginger
$1/2$ teaspoon chopped cilantro

Heat the oven to 400°F. Adjust the oven rack to the lowest position.

Stack the phyllo rounds and brush the top round with Lobster Oil. Place on a nonstick baking sheet and bake for 5 minutes. Turn over and bake for 3 minutes longer. Set aside.

Sauté the scallions in the remaining Lobster Oil until soft. Combine the remaining ingredients in a bowl and add the scallions and oil. Stir well to coat the shrimp and spread over the oiled surface of the phyllo tart. Bake for 10 minutes.

Tomato and Basil Tart

This Provençal inspiration combines fresh tomatoes, garlic, and basil on a crisp phyllo base.
Unless you are fortunate enough to have flavorful, juicy tomatoes year-round,
prepare this only in the summer months when tomatoes are at their best.

MAKES 1 TART

4 sheets phyllo dough, cut into 10-inch rounds	1/2 teaspoon chopped thyme leaves
2 tablespoons extra virgin olive oil	Salt, freshly ground pepper, and sugar to taste
3 medium tomatoes	1 tablespoon basil leaves, cut into ribbons
1/2 teaspoon chopped chili pepper	1 tablespoon freshly grated hard goat cheese or Parmesan
1/2 teaspoon chopped garlic	

Heat the oven to 400°F. Adjust the oven rack to the lowest position.

Stack the phyllo rounds and brush the top round with olive oil. Place on a nonstick baking sheet and bake for 5 minutes. Turn over and bake for 3 minutes longer. Set aside.

Blanch tomatoes in boiling salted water for about 5 seconds. Remove the skins and squeeze out the liquid and seeds. Dice the tomatoes. In an oven-proof pan, combine the tomatoes, chili pepper, garlic, thyme, and 1 tablespoon olive oil. Season with salt, pepper, and a pinch of sugar. Bake, stirring occasionally, until the tomatoes begin to turn brown and caramelize, about 20 minutes. Set aside.

Spread the tomatoes over the oiled surface of the phyllo tart. Top with basil, cheese, and remaining olive oil. Bake for 10 minutes.

Duck Bricks

A phyllo package keeps the flavor of the aromatic contents within the pastry
until the moment the crust is broken.

SERVES 4

3 tablespoons sweet butter

3 ounces fresh cépes or white button mushrooms, washed and cut into small dice

1/4 pound boneless duck

1/2 skinless, boneless half chicken breast

9 ounces uncooked foie gras or duck or chicken livers

1 ounce prosciutto

Salt and freshly ground pepper to taste

1 egg

3 sheets phyllo dough, cut into twelve 4 × 16-inch strips

2 tablespoons Truffle Vinaigrette (page 19) or Soy and Ginger Vinaigrette (page 16)

Heat the oven to 450°F. Adjust the oven rack to lowest position.

In a small sauté pan, melt 1 tablespoon butter over medium-high heat. Add the mushrooms and sauté until golden brown. Set aside and keep warm.

Cut the duck, chicken, foie gras, and prosciutto into small dice and mix together. Season with salt and pepper. Add the egg and mushrooms and mix well.

Arrange the phyllo in 4 stacks of 3 strips. Melt the remaining 2 tablespoons butter. Brush the top strips with melted butter. Mound one-fourth of the duck mixture at the end of each stack of phyllo strips. Roll phyllo up and over the stuffing to form a triangle. Brush with melted butter. Bake on a nonstick baking sheet until golden brown, about 10 minutes.

Place 1 brick on each of 4 warmed serving plates and serve with Truffle Vinaigrette.

Duck Bonbons: You will need 4 sheets of phyllo to make 18 bonbons. Heat the oven and prepare the filling as above. Cut each sheet of phyllo into 9 rectangles, 4 1/2 × 3 inches. Make the bonbons: Stack 2 rectangles and lightly brush the top strip with melted butter. Place 1 tablespoon filling at the center edge of one long side of the rectangle. Roll the dough over the filling to enclose it completely. Gently twist the ends of the dough in opposite directions to make a "bonbon" package. Lightly brush with melted butter. Bake bonbons 5 to 7 minutes, until golden brown. Serve as above.

Goat Cheese Bricks with Endive Salad

1 cup crumbled soft, white goat cheese, such as Montrachet	3 sheets phyllo dough, cut into twelve 4 × 16-inch strips
1 1/2 teaspoons chopped rosemary	2 tablespoons extra virgin olive oil or Rosemary Oil (page 41)
1 1/2 teaspoons chopped thyme	Endive Salad (recipe follows)

Heat the oven to 450°F. Adjust the oven rack to the lowest position.

Mix the cheese and herbs. Roll the mixture into four 2-inch balls. Cover and refrigerate until ready to use.

Arrange the phyllo in 4 stacks of 3 strips. Brush the top strips lightly with olive oil. Place a ball of cheese on the end of each stack of phyllo strips. Roll phyllo up and over the cheese to form a triangle. Brush tops with olive oil. Place on a nonstick baking sheet and bake until golden brown, about 10 minutes. Serve with Endive Salad.

Endive Salad

SERVES 4

3 heads endive
1/2 teaspoon fresh lemon juice
2 tablespoons peanut oil
2 teaspoons sherry vinegar
2 teaspoons cracked raw peanuts*
1 teaspoon chopped chives
Salt and freshly ground pepper to taste

Separate the endive leaves and slice into long, thin strips. Combine remaining ingredients in a bowl and mix well. Pour over endives and toss.

*To crack peanuts, simply whack with the bottom of a heavy pot.

Lamb with Wild Mushrooms

*My version of a lamb Wellington. Wrap the meat in phyllo
just before cooking to ensure the crust is crisp.*

SERVES 4

3 cups assorted fresh wild mushrooms (shiitakes, chanterelles, morels)	2 tablespoons canola oil
3 tablespoons sweet butter	Two 1-pound lamb loins
1/2 teaspoon chopped garlic	3 sheets phyllo dough, trimmed to 10 × 13 1/2-inch rectangles
1/2 teaspoon chopped shallot	1/2 cup Mushroom Syrup (page 68)
2 tablespoons chopped parsley	2 tablespoons hazelnut or extra virgin olive oil
Salt and freshly ground pepper to taste	

Heat the oven to 450°F. Adjust the oven rack to the lowest position.

Wash and finely chop mushrooms. In a medium sauté pan, melt 1 tablespoon butter over medium-high heat. Add the garlic and shallot and sauté until translucent. Add the mushrooms and cook until their liquid evaporates. Add parsley and season with salt and pepper. Set aside.

In a large pan, heat the canola oil over high heat. Add the lamb and sear 3 minutes per side.

Make 2 stacks of 3 sheets phyllo each. Melt the remaining 2 tablespoons butter and brush the top sheets lightly. Divide the mushroom mixture between the top sheets and spread it evenly, leaving a 1-inch border on all sides. Roll each lamb loin in the phyllo. Pinch the ends to enclose the mixture. Roast for 10 minutes for rare, 12 minutes for medium-rare.

In a small sauce pan, warm the Mushroom Syrup over medium-high heat. Whisk in the hazelnut oil and season with salt and pepper. Slice the lamb about 1 inch thick and serve with the sauce.

Squab Purse

SERVES 4

4 tablespoons sweet butter	12 sheets phyllo dough, cut into twenty-four 8-inch rounds
4 squab*, skinned and breasts boned	3 tablespoons hazelnut or extra virgin olive oil
8 shiitake mushrooms	$1/2$ cup Mushroom Syrup (page 68)
Salt and freshly ground pepper to taste	
Four 2-ounce slices uncooked foie gras, diced	

Heat the oven to 450°F. Adjust the oven rack to the lowest position.

In a large sauté pan, melt 2 tablespoons butter over medium-high heat. Add the squab and sauté 5 minutes per side. Cut each breast in 6 equal pieces. Cut mushrooms into pieces the same size as the breast meat.

Add 1 tablespoon butter to the pan and sauté the mushrooms until their liquid evaporates. Season with salt and pepper. Combine the sliced breast meat, mushrooms, and foie gras in a bowl.

Arrange the phyllo in 8 stacks of 3 rounds each. Melt the remaining tablespoon butter and brush over the tops of the stacks. Divide the mushroom mixture among the stacks, mounding it in the center of each. Place one squab leg on top of each. Gather the sides of each round up to the center, to form a "purse" with the leg bone peeking out the top. Secure the purses with kitchen string.

Place on a nonstick baking sheet and brush with hazelnut oil. Bake for 15 minutes.

In a small saucepan, warm the Mushroom Syrup over medium-high heat. Whisk in 2 tablespoons hazelnut oil. Season with salt and pepper.

Put 2 purses on each of 4 warmed serving plates. Serve with the sauce.

---

*You can substitute two 2- to 3-pound baby chickens for the squab. Slice all the meat into smallish pieces and add to the mushrooms. Remember to keep phyllo covered when not working with it, so it doesn't dry out.

Lobster Strudel

The filling can be prepared ahead of time, but to keep the phyllo crisp,

assemble and bake the strudel just before serving.

SERVES 4

1^1/2-pound lobster	Salt and freshly ground pepper to taste
^{1}/2 cup peeled, seeded, and diced tomato	3 sheets phyllo dough, trimmed to 8 × 12^1/2-inch rectangles
^{1}/4 cup chopped cilantro	
^{1}/2 cup Lobster Oil (page 41) or Shrimp Oil (page 42)	

Heat the oven to 450°F. Adjust the oven rack to the lowest position.

Cook the lobster in boiling salted water for 2 minutes. Drain, let cool and remove the meat from the tail and claws. Dice the lobster meat and add the tomato, cilantro, 2 tablespoons Lobster Oil, salt, and pepper.

Stack the phyllo sheets and brush the top sheet lightly with Lobster Oil. Spread the lobster mixture evenly over the phyllo, leaving a ^{1}/2- to ^{3}/4-inch border. Starting from one long side, roll the phyllo over the filling, jellyroll fashion, and brush the top of the roll with Lobster Oil. Place the roll on a nonstick baking sheet and bake for 15 minutes. Cut into 1-inch slices and serve with the remaining Lobster Oil.

Apple Tart

1 sheet phyllo dough, cut into four 6-inch rounds	3 tablespoons sweet butter, melted
1 apple, peeled and thinly sliced	1 tablespoon sugar

Heat the oven to 400°F. Adjust the oven rack to the lowest position.

Stack the phyllo rounds and brush the top round with butter. Place on a nonstick baking sheet and bake for 5 minutes.

Starting at the outside edge of the round, cover the phyllo with overlapping apple slices, arranging them in a spiral as you progress toward the center.

Drizzle 2 tablespoons butter over the apples. Sprinkle with sugar and bake for 15 minutes. Serve hot.

Foie Gras

Foie gras, the liver of a fattened goose or duck, is one of the most exquisite foods imaginable, both in flavor and in its silken texture. If calves' liver is what comes to mind when you hear the words foie gras, banish the thought; they don't resemble each other in the least. The delicacy of foie gras requires simple preparation so as not to overwhelm the very qualities that make it so luxurious. Traditionally it is combined or eaten with such rich flavors as those of port, Madeira, and Sauternes, in small amounts that embellish but don't compete.

Foie gras is not a dish for every day. It is expensive and, unfortunately, not the best for one's diet. But when I want to splurge, I can't think of anything I would rather eat.

Cold, freshly cooked foie gras (page 109) is the purest form of foie gras. When it is served, that purity should be maintained. It is best served with only toasted brioche or other good bread.

When preparing warm foie gras, an important step in finishing the sauce is adding back some of the fat the foie gras gave up when it was sautéed. This makes for a glossier, more richly flavored sauce.

Foie gras is certainly not to be found in every butcher shop. If you find it difficult to get fresh foie gras locally, you can order it from D'Artagnan in New Jersey, telephone 201-792-0748.

From my earliest days, watching Paul Haeberlin of L'Auberge de I'lll prepare foie gras and tasting the result of my master's work, I have tried to create different and new dishes of foie gras. Once you start working with foie gras, you will be amazed how easy the recipes are to prepare. I hope you truly enjoy the glorious results.

Cooked Foie Gras

This must be prepared 1 day in advance in order for the flavor to develop properly.
Let it come to room temperature before serving. Don't use a terrine mold that is too large
for the amount of foie gras to be cooked. If you have only a small amount of foie gras,
use a small casserole or even a ramekin. The foie gras should be at least 2 inches thick.

SERVES 15

2-pounds uncooked foie gras	**1 tablespoon salt**
Milk or water	**Pinch freshly ground pepper**

Heat the oven to 350°F.

Soak the foie gras in milk or water to cover for 2 hours at room temperature. Drain it, remove the nerves, and separate into 2 lobes. Season with salt and pepper.

Place the foie gras in a 1 1/2-quart ceramic terrine mold and gently press to fill any air spaces. Cover with aluminum foil. Place the mold in a deep baking pan. Pour hot water into the baking pan to reach three-fourths up the mold. Bake for about 1 hour. To test if the foie gras is done, insert a meat thermometer into the foie gras. If it reads 150°F, the foie gras is done. If not, continue to bake a little longer and test again. Remove the baking pan from oven and let the mold cool in the water. When it reaches room temperature, cover tightly and refrigerate.

Poached Foie Gras with Fennel and Caramel Pepper

This is a recipe we developed at Lafayette and it is one of my favorites.
As the "correct" wine to drink with foie gras is Sauternes, this dish boasts a perfect balance.

SERVES 4

2 medium bulbs fennel (2 cups), sliced, leaves reserved for garnish	1 bottle Sauternes, Gewürztraminer or Muscat
1 cup water	2 tablespoons sugar
1 tablespoon sweet butter	$1/2$ teaspoon cracked black pepper
Salt to taste	4 teaspoons fresh lime juice (or to taste)
Four 5-ounce slices uncooked foie gras (each about $1/2$-inch thick)	

In a medium saucepan, combine the fennel, water, and butter. Add a pinch of salt and cook over medium-high heat until all the water evaporates. Set aside and keep warm.

Put the foie gras in a sauté pan at least 10 inches wide and add Sauternes to cover. Poach over low heat (do not let it come to a boil) until Sauternes begins to simmer; cook for 2 minutes. Remove the foie gras and keep warm. Reserve the cooking liquid.

In a separate pan, melt the sugar with the pepper over medium-high heat and cook until it turns a rich brown color. Deglaze the pan with half the reserved cooking liquid. Reduce by half. Add the lime juice.

Put some of the fennel on each of 4 warmed serving plates. Top it with a slice of foie gras and pour some of the caramel sauce on top. Garnish with fennel leaves.

Marble of Foie Gras

This is a great party dish. One night at Lafayette a portion of warm foie gras came back to the kitchen. We didn't want to waste it and so it was placed in the refrigerator. We tasted it the following day and found the flavor to be fabulous. This "marble" is unusual in that it uses cooked foie gras to make a cold terrine. It is simple, easily prepared when the mold is lined with plastic wrap. If you want to use only 1 pound of foie gras, divide all ingredients in half and use an accordingly smaller mold.

SERVES 12

2-pounds uncooked foie gras	$1/4$ cup cognac or brandy
2 tablespoons paprika	$1/4$ cup green peppercorns, drained and finely chopped
Salt and freshly ground pepper to taste	
4 cups Mushroom Broth (page 68)	Corn Muffins (page 154), toasted
2 tablespoons unflavored gelatin	

Slice the foie gras $1/2$ inch thick and arrange in a single layer in a dish. Season with paprika, salt, and pepper. Cover tightly and refrigerate 2 hours.

In a medium saucepan, warm the Mushroom Broth over medium-high heat. When it is hot, sprinkle with gelatin. Stir to dissolve. Bring the broth to a boil and season with salt and pepper. Remove from the heat and set aside.

Heat a large sauté pan over high heat. When the pan is hot, add the foie gras and sauté 20 seconds per side. Remove foie gras from the pan and drain the fat. Deglaze the pan with cognac and cook until the cognac evaporates. Add the Mushroom Broth and reduce by half. Add the chopped green peppercorns and remove from the heat.

Line a $1 1/2$-quart ceramic terrine mold with plastic wrap. Arrange a layer of the foie gras in the mold and cover with broth. Continue layering, ending with broth. Cover tightly with plastic wrap and refrigerate, weighted, until the terrine is firm, at least 4 hours. Slice about $1/3$ inch thick and serve with corn muffins.

Sautéed Foie Gras and Potato Terrine

This is a signature dish created in the fall of 1988. My former sous-chef Pierre Schultz always
lined pans with thin slices of potatoes for this recipe. This dish takes a little time, but it's worth it.
The potato takes on the character of the foie gras, the foie gras the character of the potato.
When you are comfortable with one or two of the other foie gras preparations, try this dish.
You won't be disappointed. Don't add fat to the pan before sautéing slices of terrine.
The fat of the foie gras will be enough.

SERVES 12

10 medium Idaho potatoes, peeled and
   sliced 1/8 inch thick
1 cup Clarified Butter (page 196)
1 pound uncooked foie gras, cut into
   1/2-inch slices
All-purpose flour
1/2 cup Mushroom Syrup (page 68)

1/4 cup hazelnut oil
2 tablespoons sherry vinegar
Salt and freshly ground pepper to taste
1/4 cup chopped chives
Pinch coarse salt

Heat the oven to 400°F.

Dip the potato slices in Clarified Butter. Arrange in a single layer on a nonstick baking sheet. Bake until tender but remove from the oven before they take on any color, about 15 minutes. Lightly pat dry with paper toweling.

Line a 1 1/2-quart ceramic terrine mold with plastic wrap, leaving a 4-inch overhang on all sides. Line the mold with a 1/4-inch layer of potatoes on the bottom and up the sides.

Place a layer of foie gras over the potatoes. Cover foie gras with another 1/4-inch layer of potatoes, then add the remaining foie gras and finish with the remaining potatoes. Cover the mold with the overhang of plastic wrap. Weight the top of the mold and refrigerate for at least 2 hours.

Unmold the terrine and slice $1/2$ inch thick. Dust the slices with flour and shake off any excess. Heat a large nonstick pan over high heat. When the pan is very hot, add the slices of terrine and sauté about 30 seconds per side, until potato is golden brown and crisp. Remove to warmed serving plates.

Warm the Mushroom Syrup and whisk in the hazelnut oil and sherry vinegar. Remove from the heat and season with salt and pepper.

Sprinkle chives around each plate. Sprinkle a pinch of coarse salt on each slice of terrine and a turn of fresh pepper from a pepper mill. Pour a little of the sauce around each plate and serve.

Foie Gras with Fried Leeks

SERVES 4

1-pound uncooked foie gras, cut into 4 slices	1 tablespoon cracked black pepper
Salt and freshly ground pepper to taste	2 tablespoons cracked raw peanuts*
2 tablespoons sherry vinegar	2 tablespoons chopped chives
2 cups Mushroom Broth (page 68)	
3 tablespoons Peanut Oil (page 43) or commercial peanut oil	*garnish* Leek Julienne (page 198)

Heat a medium sauté pan over high heat. When the pan is hot, add the foie gras and sauté for 1 1/2 minutes per side. Remove foie gras from the pan and place on individual plates. Season with salt and pepper and cover to keep warm.

Drain excess fat from the pan. Deglaze the pan with vinegar and cook until the vinegar evaporates. Add the Mushroom Broth and reduce to a syrup (no more than 1/2 cup). Whisk in the Peanut Oil (the oil will separate from the rest of the sauce). Keep warm.

Sprinkle the cracked pepper, peanuts, and chives around the foie gras. Top the foie gras with fried leeks and spoon a little sauce around the plate.

*To crack peanuts, give them one or two whacks with the bottom of a heavy pot.

Foie Gras with Ginger and Mango

The traditional Outhier warm foie gras dish combines foie gras with apples and sorrel.
When I was sent to Thailand and couldn't find apples, I used mangoes instead.

SERVES 4

2 ripe mangoes	$1/2$ cup dry white wine
1 tablespoon powdered sugar	1 tablespoon fresh ginger julienne
Four $1^1/2$-inch slices uncooked foie gras (4 ounces each)	1 teaspoon fresh lime juice
	Salt and freshly ground pepper to taste
2 cups fresh orange juice	

Peel the mangoes and cut the flesh away from the pits in 2 large halves each. Cut each half from the top nearly to the bottom into 4 long slices. Fan the slices. Sprinkle one side of each fan with sugar and cook, sugar side down, in a nonstick pan over medium-high heat until caramelized. Place on serving plates, caramel side up.

Heat a small sauté pan over medium-high heat until hot. Add the foie gras and cook $1^1/2$ minutes per side. Remove from the pan and keep warm. Deglaze the pan with orange juice, white wine, and ginger. Reduce to a syrup and add lime juice and any fat given off by the foie gras. Season with salt and pepper. Place the foie gras next to the mango fans and spoon some of the sauce over it.

Foie Gras with Figs

This is very simple and the flavor is unique.

If you want to make the roulade quickly, though, substitute good-quality prosciutto.

SERVES 6

Air-dried Duck Breast (recipe follows) or **1 pound thinly sliced prosciutto**	36 leaves mäche or arugula
7 ounces Cooked Foie Gras (page 109), **left at room temperature until soft**	1 teaspoon cracked black pepper
6 fresh figs	Port Wine Aspic (recipe follows)
	1 tablespoon chives, cut into 1/2-inch lengths

Slice duck breasts very thin. Spread a sheet of aluminum foil over a kitchen surface. Arrange the sliced duck on the foil in a single layer. Spread with foie gras and roll into a cylinder. Wrap in the foil and twist the ends tightly. Refrigerate until firm, about 2 hours.

Slice roulade and the figs approximately 1/4 inch thick. Alternate 3 slices of each on serving plates. Garnish with mäche leaves. Scatter the pepper, aspic, and chives over all.

Air-Dried Duck Breast

1-pound whole duck breast, skinned
6 coriander seeds, cracked
1 bay leaf
1 bunch thyme
1 tablespoon coarse salt
6 black peppercorns

Rub the duck breast with the remaining ingredients, cover loosely, and let sit for 24 hours. Hang it in cheesecloth in a cool, well-ventilated place to cure for 15 days.

Port Wine Aspic

1 bottle port wine
$1^1/2$ tablespoons unflavored gelatin

Heat the port until hot. Sprinkle the gelatin over the port and stir to dissolve thoroughly. Pour into a jelly roll pan and refrigerate until firm, about $1^1/2$ hours. Cut into small dice.

Soufflé of Foie Gras

This dish is fabulously rich and needs no sauce. Serve with a glass of Sauternes or champagne.

SERVES 4

1 tablespoon sweet butter	Generous $^1/4$ cup uncooked foie gras, for
1 tablespoon all-purpose flour	purée
4 eggs, separated	Pinch salt
$^1/4$ cup truffle juice* or slightly reduced	Pinch cream of tartar
Mushroom Broth (page 68)	$^1/2$ cup diced uncooked foie gras

Heat the oven to 500°F.

Butter and flour four 4-ounce ceramic ramekins and set them in the freezer.

Beat together the egg yolks and truffle juice in the top of a double boiler set over—not touching—boiling water. Whisk until light and fluffy. Let cool to room temperature.

Pass $^1/4$ cup foie gras through a sieve to purée. Mix the purée into the egg mixture. Beat the egg whites with salt and cream of tartar until stiff. Fold gently into the foie gras mixture, then pour into each ramekin until half full. Divide the diced foie gras among the ramekins, then fill them with the remaining soufflé mixture. Place the ramekins in a deep baking dish. Add hot water to reach halfway up the ramekins. Cook for 15 minutes and serve immediately.

*Available in cans from specialty stores and gourmet shops. The liquid in which canned or jarred truffles are packed may be used.

On an
Asian Note

When I joined Louis Outhier's "flying squadron of chefs," a large part of my time from 1981 to 1983 was spent in East Asia: Bangkok, Hong Kong, and Singapore. The flavors and subtleties of the ingredients and spices of East Asia brought a new dimension to my cooking.

The recipes that follow are a marriage of the influences of East Asia and France. They aren't intended to be used exclusively as part of "Eastern" menus, and are exquisite with and often enhanced by Western flavors. As you will see, many of the recipes call for one or two seemingly exotic "Eastern" ingredients. All can be obtained in Asian markets throughout the United States.

Eggs with Oysters

SERVES 4

1/2 cup heavy cream, whipped	1 tablespoon sesame seeds
1/2 tablespoon wasabi powder*, mixed to a paste with 1/2 tablespoon water	2 tablespoons sweet butter
	4 eggs
Salt and cayenne pepper to taste	8 large, fresh oysters, coarsely chopped

Heat the oven to 250°F.

Combine the whipped cream and wasabi paste. Season with salt and cayenne pepper and mix well. Refrigerate until needed.

Spread sesame seeds on a baking sheet and bake until they are lightly toasted.

Melt 1 tablespoon butter in a small saucepan over medium-low heat. In a medium bowl, whisk together the eggs, salt, and cayenne pepper. Add to the saucepan and cook, stirring constantly with a wooden spoon until eggs scramble; add the remaining 1 tablespoon butter toward the end of cooking. They should be fairly loose, not dry.

Divide the eggs among 4 ramekins. Top with chopped oysters and cover with a spoonful of wasabi cream. Sprinkle sesame seeds over the cream and serve.

*Wasabi powder may be purchased in an Asian market featuring Japanese products. It has a flavor similar to that of horseradish.

Tempura with Cabbage Salad
and Cinnamon Oil

SERVES 4

3 cups shredded Chinese cabbage (about 1/4 pound)	Salt and cayenne pepper to taste
1 teaspoon honey	2 tablespoons cornstarch
1/4 cup rice vinegar	2 tablespoons water
1 teaspoon cracked green coriander seeds	32 large shrimp, peeled to the tail and deveined
1 teaspoon grated lemon zest	1 1/2 cups canola oil
1 teaspoon grated orange zest	1/4 cup Cinnamon Oil (page 39)
1 teaspoon chopped fresh ginger	

Toss the cabbage thoroughly with honey, vinegar, coriander, zests, ginger, salt, and cayenne pepper. Cover and let stand at room temperature for at least 1 hour.

Combine the cornstarch and water and mix well. In a large sauté pan or Chinese wok, heat the oil to 375°F. Dip shrimp into cornstarch mixture and fry until crisp, about 1 minute. Season with salt and cayenne pepper. Serve with the cabbage salad and sprinkle Cinnamon Oil over all.

Veal in Rice Paper

When you have used rice paper just once, you will be eager to experiment. It can be used as a wrapper for all kinds of fillings. Try sautéed foie gras and apples with Curry Oil (page 39) or chopped, uncooked shrimp with cilantro, scallions, and Shrimp Oil (page 42). Rice paper packages may be lightly fried in a tablespoon of peanut or sesame oil in a nonstick pan.

SERVES 4

2 tablespoons sweet butter	1 tablespoon fresh lemon juice
1 1/4 pounds veal (top round), cut into large dice	2 tablespoons nam pla[*] (fish sauce)
2 cups chanterelle or shiitake mushrooms	Salt and freshly ground pepper to taste
1 tablespoon finely chopped fresh ginger	3 tablespoons chopped cilantro
3 tablespoons sliced scallions	Four 8-inch sheets rice paper[*]
2 tablespoons soy sauce	1/4 cup Soy and Ginger Vinaigrette (page 16), warmed

Melt the butter in a large sauté pan over medium-high heat. Add the veal and sauté until light brown, 5 to 7 minutes. Season with salt and pepper.

Wash the mushrooms and lightly pat dry. Cut any large mushrooms in half. Add mushrooms, ginger, and scallions to veal. Cook until mushroom liquid evaporates, about 5 minutes.

Deglaze the pan with soy sauce, lemon juice, and nam pla. Bring to a boil and remove from heat. Season with salt and pepper and stir in the cilantro.

Soften each round of rice paper between layers of damp kitchen toweling for about 5 minutes, until pliable enough to roll without cracking, but not wet. Divide the veal mixture among the rounds, mounding it in the center of each. Fold the rice paper around the mixture to form a rectangular packet. Steam packets over boiling water for 5 minutes. Serve with warm Soy and Ginger Vinaigrette.

[*]*Nam pla and rice paper are sold in Asian markets.*

Thai Shrimp Cakes

My version of Tod Mon Pla. Nam pla is a fish sauce that can be purchased in Asian markets.

SERVES 4

1 stalk lemongrass, chopped	1 teaspoon honey
1 cup boiling water	2 tablespoons cracked raw peanuts*
1 pound medium shrimp, peeled and deveined	1/4 cup cucumber, seeded and diced
2 tablespoons sliced scallions	1 medium chili pepper, finely chopped
1 tablespoon chopped cilantro	2 tablespoons peanut oil, homemade or commercial
Salt and cayenne pepper to taste	2 tablespoons sweet butter
1/4 cup nam pla (fish sauce)	2 tablespoons canola oil
2 tablespoons plus 2 teaspoons fresh lime juice	*garnish* Sliced scallions and chopped cilantro

Put the lemongrass in a bowl and cover with boiling water. Let infuse for 10 minutes. Strain the liquid and let cool to room temperature.

In a food processor or blender, combine the shrimp with 1/2 cup of the infusion. Process until nearly smooth but still somewhat chunky. Transfer to a bowl and stir in scallions and cilantro. Season with salt and cayenne pepper. Set aside.

Combine the remaining ingredients except the butter, canola oil, and garnish. Set aside.

Heat the butter and canola oil in a nonstick pan over medium-high heat. Drop large tablespoonfuls of shrimp mixture into the pan and flatten them slightly into 2-inch cakes. Cook about 30 seconds per side until golden brown. Pool some of the sauce on each serving plate and top with the shrimp cakes. Garnish with scallions and cilantro.

To crack peanuts, give them one or two whacks with the bottom of a heavy pan.

Rice Paper Sushi

This sushi is served cold, a perfect appetizer or summer dish. The flavors come together nicely during refrigeration. It may be prepared up to six hours in advance, but let it sit at room temperature for 3 to 5 minutes before serving. Rounds of rice paper and wasabi powder are available at most Asian markets. This roll reminds me of futomaki or a California roll.

SERVES 2

Two 8-inch sheets rice paper	2 or 3 slices avocado
1/2 cup bean sprouts	1 tablespoon cilantro leaves
Lightly cooked seafood: 1/2 small lobster, 5 medium sea scallops, 5 medium shrimp, or a thin slice of cod (3 to 4 ounces)	Spiced Soy Sauce (recipe follows)

Soften each round of rice paper between layers of damp kitchen toweling for about 5 minutes until pliable enough to roll without cracking, but not wet.

Place a sheet of plastic wrap on a clean kitchen surface. Stack the softened rounds of rice paper on the plastic wrap.

Arrange bean sprouts in a line about one third of the way across the rice paper, reaching all the way to the edges. Place the fish or shellfish over the sprouts and top with slices of avocado. Sprinkle with cilantro.

Roll the rice paper and its contents tightly into a long roll (leave the ends open). Wrap the roll tightly in plastic, twisting the ends to make an airtight package.

Refrigerate for at least 1 hour. When ready to serve, unwrap and cut into 2-inch pieces. Serve with Spiced Soy Sauce.

Spiced Soy Sauce

$1/2$ cup soy sauce

1 teaspoon wasabi powder

1 tablespoon minced fresh ginger

1 tablespoon sake

1 tablespoon rice wine vinegar

1 tablespoon dark sesame oil or peanut oil

Combine all ingredients.

Sweetbread Fritters
with Ginger Vinaigrette

1/2 pound sweetbreads	3/4 cup water
1 3/4 cups all-purpose flour	3 egg whites
1 1/2 cups plus 1 tablespoon canola oil	Salt
1 whole egg	3/4 cup Ginger Vinaigrette (page 16)
3 tablespoons beer	2 tablespoons chopped cilantro

Put the sweetbreads in cold salted water and bring the water to a boil. Drain the sweetbreads and remove the nerves. Cut into large dice. Refrigerate until needed.

Combine flour, 1 tablespoon oil, whole egg, beer, and water and mix well. Beat the egg whites with a pinch of salt to stiff peaks. Fold into the beer batter.

In a Chinese wok or large sauté pan, heat the remaining 1 1/2 cups oil until very hot (315°F). Dip the diced sweetbreads into the batter. Fry about 2 minutes, until golden brown on all sides. Drain on paper toweling and sprinkle with salt.

Combine the Ginger Vinaigrette and cilantro. Serve with the sweetbread fritters.

Grilled Pig's Feet with Peanuts

Don't be put off—try this one! This Thai-inspired dish is simple and truly wonderful.

SERVES 4

4 cooked pig's feet (purchase from a butcher)	2 tablespoons peanut oil, homemade or commercial
2 tablespoons cracked raw peanuts	1/4 cup Dijon mustard
2 tablespoons unseasoned breadcrumbs, fresh or commercial	

Put the pig's feet in a pot and add enough water to cover them halfway. Cook over medium heat for 10 minutes. Drain and remove the bones. Press the meat into espresso-size cups lined with plastic wrap. Cover tightly and refrigerate overnight.

Heat the oven to 550°F.

Mix together the peanuts and breadcrumbs. Carefully remove the meat from the cups and brush with oil and mustard. Roll in the breadcrumb mixture. Place on a baking sheet and bake for 20 minutes. Place under a preheated broiler until the crust browns. Serve with a mixed salad or Endive Salad (page 103).

Lacquered Bacon

$^1/_2$ medium carrot, peeled

$^1/_2$ medium onion, peeled

$^1/_2$ medium leek, washed thoroughly

2 pounds raw, unsmoked, and unsliced bacon

1 Bouquet Garni (page 196)

$^1/_4$ cup honey

$^1/_4$ cup vinegar (rice wine, white wine, or any other white vinegar)

Honey-Ginger Glazed Shallots (recipe follows)

Cut the vegetables into large cubes. Put the vegetables, bacon, and Bouquet Garni in a pot with water to cover. Bring to a boil and reduce heat. Simmer for 1 hour.

Drain the bacon and cut into large cubes. Discard the vegetables and liquid.

In a medium sauté pan, heat the honey over medium-high heat until caramelized. Deglaze the pan with vinegar. Add the bacon and cook, stirring constantly, until bacon is well coated. Serve with Honey-Ginger Glazed Shallots.

Honey-Ginger Glazed Shallots

$1^1/_2$ cups medium shallots, peeled and thinly sliced

2 tablespoons fresh ginger julienne

$^1/_4$ cup honey

$^1/_3$ cup red wine vinegar

$^1/_2$ cup water

$^1/_4$ teaspoon cracked black pepper

Salt to taste

In a medium saucepan, combine the shallots, ginger, and honey. Cook over medium-high heat about 5 minutes, until caramelized. Deglaze the pan with vinegar and cook until the vinegar evaporates. Add the water and reduce heat to medium-low. Cook until nearly dry. Stir in the cracked pepper, and season with salt.

Thai Chicken Soup
with Coconut Milk

SERVES 4

2 tablespoons sweet butter	2 tablespoons sliced scallions
1/4 cup chopped onion	2 tablespoons peeled, seeded, and diced tomato
2 tablespoons chopped lemongrass	2 tablespoons chopped cilantro
2 tablespoons chopped fresh ginger	1 cup coconut milk*
1/2 teaspoon red pepper flakes	1 cup button mushrooms, cut into large dice
1 chili pepper, seeded, deribbed, and chopped	2 tablespoons nam pla* (fish sauce)
4 cups Mixed Vegetable Broth (page 68)	Salt to taste
2 whole chicken breasts, skinned and boned	

Melt the butter in a large sauté pan over medium-high heat.

Add the onion, lemongrass, ginger, red pepper flakes, and chili pepper, and cook until onion is translucent. Add Mixed Vegetable Broth and cook for 10 minutes. Add chicken breasts and poach for 5 minutes. Remove the chicken and strain the liquid, discarding the solids. Cut the chicken into large dice and place in a large soup tureen. Add scallions, tomato, and cilantro to the tureen.

Heat the strained liquid with the coconut milk and mushrooms and bring to a boil. Stir in nam pla and cook for 5 minutes. Season with salt. Add the broth to the tureen.

*Nam pla is fish sauce that can be purchased in Asian markets. Coconut milk is not the liquid inside coconuts. It can be found in gourmet shops and markets specializing in Latin and Asian groceries. Be sure not to buy sweetened coconut milk or coconut cream.

Shrimp and Chicken
in Lemongrass Broth

3 cups water	$3/4$ cup button mushrooms, cut into small dice
1 large chili pepper, seeded, deribbed, and chopped	$1/4$ cup sliced scallions
2 stalks lemongrass, chopped	2 tablespoons chopped cilantro
2 whole chicken breasts, skinned and boned	$1/2$ teaspoon fresh lemon juice
24 medium shrimp, peeled and deveined	Grated zest of $1/2$ lime
2 tablespoons plus 1 teaspoon nam pla* (fish sauce)	Cooked white rice

In a large pot, boil the water, chili pepper, and lemongrass for 10 minutes.

Cut the chicken into pieces the same size as the shrimp. Add the chicken and shrimp to the broth. Boil until done, about 5 minutes.

In a soup tureen, combine the remaining ingredients. Add the broth, chicken, and shrimp to the tureen. Ladle into serving bowls over cooked white rice.

*Nam pla is a fish sauce that can be purchased in Asian markets.

Warm Shrimp Salad
with Bean Sprouts

SERVES 4

8 button mushrooms, cleaned and quartered	24 large shrimp, peeled and deveined
2 tablespoons fresh lemon juice	1 shallot, peeled and finely chopped
2 tablespoons plain yogurt	3 tablespoons soy sauce
1/4 cup heavy cream, whipped	1 cup bean sprouts
Salt and freshly ground pepper to taste	2 tablespoons raw soy nuts or peanuts
2 tablespoons sweet butter	3 tablespoons peanut oil

In a small bowl, combine the mushrooms, lemon juice, yogurt, and whipped cream. Season with salt and pepper. Set aside.

Melt the butter in a large sauté pan over medium-high heat. Add the shrimp and sauté until half cooked, about 45 seconds per side. Add the shallot and soy sauce. Bring to a boil, remove from the heat, and transfer to a bowl. Toss in the bean sprouts, soy nuts, and peanut oil. Season with salt and pepper.

Arrange the mushrooms like 3 spokes on a plate. Mound the shrimp mixture between the spokes and spoon some of the cooking liquid over them.

Lobster with Thai Spices

This was one of the first Asian dishes created by Louis Outhier, and it is still one of my favorites.

SERVES 4

Four 1¹/2-pound lobsters	¹/2 cup white port
4 tablespoons sweet butter	¹/4 apple, peeled and julienned
¹/2 teaspoon shrimp paste*	¹/4 teaspoon turmeric
¹/2 teaspoon curry paste*	¹/4 cup heavy cream, whipped
¹/3 medium carrot, peeled and julienned	1 tablespoon chopped cilantro
Pinch salt	Salt and freshly ground pepper to taste

Blanch the lobsters in boiling salted water for 2 minutes. Drain. When cool enough to handle, carefully remove the meat in one piece from the claws and tails. Set aside.

Melt 2 tablespoons butter in small saucepan over medium-high heat. Add the shrimp and curry pastes and sauté 20 seconds. Add the carrot and a pinch of salt and sauté 20 seconds. Deglaze the pan with port and add the apple. Cook until almost dry. Add the turmeric and mix well. Stir in the whipped cream and bring to a boil. Remove from the heat and add cilantro and salt to taste. Keep warm.

Melt the remaining 2 tablespoons butter in a large sauté pan. Add the lobster meat and sauté for 2 minutes. Season with salt and pepper, and serve napped with the sauce.

*Shrimp and curry pastes can be purchased in Asian markets.

Lobster Poached
in Lemongrass Broth

SERVES 4

Four 1 1/2-pound lobsters	8 button mushrooms, sliced
3 cups water	4 scallions, sliced
2 stalks lemongrass*, coarsely chopped	2 tablespoons fresh lime juice
1/2 chili pepper, seeded, deribbed, and chopped	2 tablespoons nam pla* (fish sauce)
6 sprigs plus 2 tablespoons chopped cilantro	

Blanch the lobsters in boiling salted water for 2 minutes. Drain. When cool enough to handle, remove the heads, claws, and tails. Carefully remove the meat in one piece from the claws and tails. Set aside.

Put the shells and heads in a pot. Cover with water and add lemongrass, chili pepper, and cilantro sprigs. Bring to a boil, reduce heat, and simmer for 10 minutes. Strain into a clean saucepan.

Add the lobster meat to the strained broth with mushrooms and scallions. Simmer for 3 minutes over medium-low heat. Stir in the lime juice, nam pla, and chopped cilantro.

*Nam pla is a fish sauce that can be purchased in Asian markets. Lemongrass is also available in Asian markets, especially those that feature Thai ingredients.

Black Bass in
Zucchini Blossoms

This dish combines the Provençal idea of a fish-stuffed zucchini blossom with the Asian flavor of cardamom. It would be very nice served with sautéed sliced zucchini. Zucchini blossoms can be hard to find. Lettuce leaves, blanched 20 seconds in boiling salted water, may be used to wrap the fish instead.

SERVES 4

Four 6-ounce black bass fillets	2 tablespoons cracked green cardamom seeds
Salt and cayenne pepper to taste	
12 large (about 4 inches long) zucchini blossoms, pistils and stamens removed	3 tablespoons sweet butter
	2 tablespoons fresh lemon juice
3 cups Mixed Vegetable Broth (page 68)	

Put bass into 12 equal pieces and season with salt and cayenne pepper. Stuff a piece of fish into each blossom. Steam over boiling water for 5 minutes. Remove from the steamer and keep warm.

In a medium saucepan, bring the Mixed Vegetable Broth to a boil over medium-high heat and add cardamom seeds. Reduce to 3/4 cup. Whisk in the butter and lemon juice. Season with salt and pepper. Serve over the stuffed blossoms.

Lacquered Quail with Sesame Seeds

Sometimes the simplest dishes are the best: a perfect marriage of East and West.

SERVES 4

1/2 cup honey	3 tablespoons fresh lime juice
1/2 cup soy sauce	1/2 cup water
1/4 scallion, sliced	2 tablespoons sesame seeds
Freshly ground pepper to taste	Spiced Rice (page 156)
8 quail or two 2- to 3-pound baby chickens	

Heat the oven to 550°F.

Mix the honey, soy sauce, scallion, and pepper. Add the quail and stir to coat. Let them marinate for 15 minutes.

Remove the quail from the marinade and roast for 12 to 15 minutes, until juices run clear (if using baby chickens, roast for 20 to 25 minutes). Reserve the marinade.

Remove quail to a broiler-proof dish. Deglaze the roasting pan with lime juice, water, and 1/4 cup of the marinade over medium-high heat. Reduce until the sauce is thick enough to coat a spoon. Coat the quail with sauce. Sprinkle sesame seeds over the quail and place them under a preheated broiler until piping hot; seeds should be golden brown. Serve with Spiced Rice and some of the sauce.

Chicken with Lime and Honey

Zest of 1 lime, julienned

5 tablespoons sweet butter

One 3-pound chicken, cut into serving
pieces

1 tablespoon thinly sliced fresh ginger

1 tablespoon honey

$^1/_2$ cup water

2 tablespoons fresh lime juice

Salt and freshly ground pepper to taste

2 tablespoons chopped cilantro

Corn Pancakes (page 155)

Heat the oven to 550°F.

Blanch the lime zest in boiling water for 10 seconds. Drain and set aside.

Melt the butter in a large oven-proof pan over medium-high heat. Add the chicken and sauté until golden brown, about 5 minutes per side. Add the ginger and honey and stir well to coat. Roast for 15 minutes until caramelized. Add the water and roast for 3 minutes longer, until juices run clear when chicken is pricked. Add the lime juice and season with salt and pepper.

Arrange the chicken on a warmed serving platter and pour the sauce on top. Sprinkle with chopped cilantro and lime zest. Serve with Corn Pancakes.

Potatoes, Cheese, and Other Indulgences

HERE YOU WILL FIND POTATOES TO SUIT ALL TASTES. FROM MY POINT OF VIEW, IT IS HARD TO IMAGINE A DISH THAT POTATOES, IN ONE FORM OR ANOTHER, WON'T ACCOMPANY BEAUTIFULLY AND—MAYBE—MAKE even better.

Rich potatoes, crisp potatoes, exotic potatoes, I love them all. This chapter is much more than a collection of my favorite potatoes, though. Some recipes feature cheeses or vegetables, some are for unusual soups and breads. Many of the recipes are as perfect for first courses and light lunches as they are for side dishes. And, most of them are very easy.

Potato and Basil Purée

3 medium Idaho potatoes, peeled, rinsed, and cut into large pieces	Salt
3/4 cup milk, warmed	15 large basil leaves
	6 tablespoons extra virgin olive oil

Heat the oven to 550°F.

Cook potatoes in boiling salted water until tender when pierced with a fork, 15 to 20 minutes. Drain potatoes and spread them out on a baking sheet. Dry in the oven for 7 to 10 minutes, until they whiten slightly and no longer look moist on the surface. Mash potatoes by hand with a potato masher or fork. Add milk and beat until smooth. Season with salt. Set aside and keep warm.

Blanch basil leaves in boiling salted water for 20 seconds. Drain and immediately refresh under cold running water. Lightly pat dry and put in a blender. Add olive oil and blend until very smooth.

Add basil purée to the potatoes and mix well. Heat thoroughly and serve.

Pommes Annette

4 large Idaho potatoes, peeled, rinsed, and turned (trimmed in smooth ovals)	1/4 cup Clarified Butter (page 196)
Salt	2 teaspoons sweet butter

Heat the oven to 550°F. Adjust the oven rack to the lowest position.

Slice the potatoes into coins as thin as possible. Put in a colander and sprinkle with salt. Let sit until potatoes give up some of their liquid, about 5 minutes.

Toss the potatoes in Clarified Butter to coat. Space 4 potato slices apart on a nonstick baking sheet. Fan potatoes in a circle around each of the 4 slices to make four 4-inch round "tarts." Cover the center of each with 1 final slice of potato and top each with 1/2 teaspoon butter. Cook until the potatoes are golden brown, about 45 minutes. Drain any excess butter and carefully transfer to warmed plates.

Potato Ravioli

1/2 cup canola oil

2 large Idaho potatoes, peeled and sliced lengthwise as thin as possible

1/4 cup sweet butter

1/2 medium carrot, peeled and cut into small dice

1/2 medium turnip, peeled and cut into small dice

1/2 medium zucchini, cut into small dice

1/2 medium knob celeriac, peeled and cut into small dice

1 medium truffle, cut into small dice

Salt and freshly ground pepper to taste

4 egg yolks

Heat the oven to 400°F.

Lightly brush a nonstick baking sheet with canola oil. Arrange potato slices on the baking sheet in a single layer and brush with oil. Bake until tender, about 5 to 7 minutes; do not let the potatoes take on any color. Lightly pat potatoes dry with paper toweling.

Melt the butter in a medium sauté pan over medium-high heat. Add the diced vegetables and sauté until crisp-tender, about 2 minutes. Season with salt and pepper.

Beat the egg yolks. Brush one side of the potatoes lightly with egg yolk. Mound about 1 teaspoon of the diced vegetables on half of each potato and fold over to form a raviolo. Press firmly around the edges to secure. Cover and refrigerate until ready to cook.

Heat the oil until very hot (350° to 375°F). Add the potato ravioli and fry until golden brown on all sides, about 45 seconds. Serve hot.

Goat Cheese
with Watercress Oil

This cheese makes a delicious, simple appetizer with country bread, toasted or left plain.
Served with nuts and dried fruits, it's a very nice way to end a meal, too. If you like,
roll the mixture into a log, then slice when it is chilled and firm.

SERVES 4

3/4 pound soft, white goat cheese (such as Montrachet)

1/4 cup crème fraîche or sour cream

1 tablespoon chopped chervil

1 tablespoon chopped chives

1 chili pepper, seeded, deribbed, and finely chopped

Freshly ground pepper to taste

1 tablespoon Watercress Oil (page 45)

Mix the goat cheese, crème fraîche, herbs, chili pepper, and ground pepper until smooth. Shape into 4 thick patties. Cover and refrigerate until ready to use. Place on small serving plates and drizzle with Watercress Oil.

Millefeuille of Roquefort and Boursin

1/2 cup Roquefort, at room temperature	1 tablespoon chopped chives
1/2 cup Boursin or cream cheese, at room temperature	Salt and freshly ground pepper to taste
1 tablespoon sweet butter	3 sheets phyllo dough, trimmed to 8 × 8-inch squares
1/2 teaspoon cognac or brandy	3 tablespoons sweet butter, melted
1/2 cup heavy cream, whipped	1 tablespoon Chive Oil (page 43)

Heat the oven to 450°F. Adjust the oven rack to the lowest position.

Combine Roquefort, Boursin, and 1 tablespoon butter in a food processor or blender and process until smooth. Transfer to a bowl and fold in cognac, whipped cream, chives, salt, and pepper. Mix thoroughly. Set aside at room temperature.

Stack the 3 sheets of phyllo on a nonstick baking sheet. Lightly brush the top sheet with melted butter. Bake until golden brown, 5 to 7 minutes. Let cool.

Cut a 2 × 8-inch strip from the phyllo and set aside. Spread or pipe the cheese mixture evenly over the large phyllo sheet. Refrigerate until firm, about 1 hour. When firm, cut into three 2 × 8-inch strips. Stack the strips one on top of the other. Top with the reserved strip. Warm in the oven for 30 seconds. Cut into serving pieces. Serve with a sprinkling of Chive Oil.

Truffled Brie

Two 1-pound rounds ripe brie	2 medium truffles, finely chopped
1 pound mascarpone or sour cream	$1/4$ cup truffle juice[*]

Trim off and discard the top rind from each round of brie. Combine the remaining ingredients and spread the mixture smoothly over the cut surface of one round. Cover with the other round, cut surface down. Cover tightly and refrigerate overnight. Bring to room temperature (about $1/2$ hour) before serving.

Mushroom Duxelles: Mince $1/2$ pound of button mushrooms, shiitake mushrooms, or morels. Saute in $1/4$ cup extra virgin olive oil over medium-high heat until all but $1/2$ cup of their liquid has evaporated. Add 2 tablespoons chopped chives and let cool. When cool, stir in the mascarpone.

[*]*Truffle juice can be purchased in cans. You may also use the liquid in which jarred or canned truffles are packed. Substitute a duxelle of fresh mushrooms for the truffle and truffle juice, if you prefer.*

Cheese Galette with Pecans

SERVES 4

5 ounces Port-Salut, at room temperature	1 egg, beaten
$1/2$ cup Roquefort, at room temperature	1 cup pecans, finely chopped, plus 4 whole pecans for garnish
5 tablespoons sweet butter	

Combine the cheeses and 3 tablespoons butter in a food processor or blender. Process until smooth. Shape into 4 patties, about $3/4$ inch thick. Dip into beaten egg and then into chopped pecans to coat. Melt 2 tablespoons butter in a medium sauté pan over medium-high heat. Add the patties and cook until golden brown, about $1^1/2$ minutes per side. Garnish with whole pecans.

Broccoli Mousse
with Truffle Vinaigrette

This melt-in-your-mouth mousse can be served as a starter or side dish.

SERVES 4

1 pound broccoli, trimmed and cut into chunks

$1/4$ teaspoon unflavored gelatin

$1/4$ cup heavy cream, whipped

Salt and freshly ground pepper to taste

2 tablespoons Truffle Vinaigrette (page 19), Peanut Vinaigrette (page 18), or Hazelnut Vinaigrette (page 18)

Cook the broccoli in boiling salted water until tender, 6 to 8 minutes. Drain and place in a food processor or blender. Process to a smooth purée. Sprinkle gelatin over the purée and process for 5 seconds. Transfer to a bowl and fold in the whipped cream thoroughly. Season with salt and pepper.

Pour into 4 well-buttered 3- or 4-ounce ramekins. Cover tightly and refrigerate until set. About 2 hours. Unmold by running a sharp knife around the inside rim. Serve with the Truffle Vinaigrette.

Wild Mushroom Gâteau

If the varieties of mushrooms called for are not available, just use as many different varieties as you can find. The greater the variety of mushrooms, the more distinctive the flavor will be.

SERVES 8

Crêpes (recipe follows)   1 cup Hazelnut Vinaigrette (page 18)
Mushroom Duxelles (recipe follows)

Heat the oven to 400°F. Divide the Mushroom Duxelles among 7 of the Crêpes and spread evenly over each, right to the edges. Neatly stack the filled crepes and place the plain crêpe on the top. Transfer to a baking sheet and warm in the oven for about 10 minutes. Serve with Hazelnut Vinaigrette.

Crêpes

MAKES 8 CREPES

1/4 cup sweet butter
1 cup all-purpose flour
3 eggs
1 cup milk
Pinch salt

Melt the butter in a small saucepan and cook until golden brown. Let cool until just warm.

Put the flour in a large mixing bowl. Add the eggs, milk, and salt. Whisk well until batter is smooth and has no lumps. Whisk in the butter thoroughly. Cover the batter and let it rest in the refrigerator for 20 minutes.

Heat a 4- to 5-inch nonstick pan over medium-high heat. When hot, pour in just enough batter to cover the bottom of the pan. Cook until golden, then turn over to cook the other side (cook about 30 seconds per side). Repeat until you have 8 crêpes. Stack crêpes as they are made.

Mushroom Duxelles

1 cup chanterelle mushrooms
1 cup black trumpet mushrooms
1 cup button mushrooms
1 cup shiitake mushrooms
1 tablespoon sweet butter
1 clove garlic, peeled and chopped
1 shallot, peeled and chopped
Salt and freshly ground pepper to taste
1 tablespoon chopped chervil
1 tablespoon chopped chives

Wash and finely chop the mushrooms. Melt the butter in a medium sauté pan over medium-high heat. Add the garlic and shallot and cook until translucent. Add the mushrooms, salt, and pepper. Reduce heat to medium and cook until the mushroom liquid evaporates. Transfer to a medium mixing bowl. Stir in the chervil and chives.

Swiss Chard Timbales

Swiss chard has a pronounced flavor that is superb with roast meats and chicken.

SERVES 4

1 pound Swiss chard, washed thoroughly and tough stems discarded	2 cups heavy cream
1 cup water	2 tablespoons freshly ground Parmesan
2 tablespoons fresh lemon juice	1 egg yolk
Pinch salt	Salt, freshly ground pepper, and freshly ground nutmeg to taste
2 cloves garlic, peeled and chopped	

Put the white part of Swiss chard into small dice. Reserve the greens.

In a large pot, bring the water to a boil with lemon juice and a pinch of salt. Add the diced Swiss chard and simmer until tender, about 10 minutes. Drain and set aside. Blanch the greens in boiling salted water until soft, less than 1 minute. Drain and set aside.

In a medium saucepan, combine the garlic and the cream. Reduce over medium heat by three-fourths. Add Parmesan, egg yolk, salt, pepper, and nutmeg. Add diced Swiss chard and mix well.

Line 4 espresso-size cups or 2-ounce ramekins with plastic wrap. Line the plastic completely with greens, leaving an overhang around the top. Fill cups with the cream mixture and fold the greens over the top. Cover tightly with plastic wrap. Steam for 15 minutes. Unmold and serve.

Bouillon with Basil Dumplings

This is my version of a Provençal soupe au pistou, a vegetable soup with a garnish of basil-scented purée.

SERVES 4

2 tablespoons extra virgin olive oil	6 cups water
1 medium carrot, peeled and diced	1 Bouquet Garni (page 196)
1 medium onion, peeled and diced	$1/2$ cup fresh or frozen peas
1 medium leek, washed thoroughly and diced	12 string beans
	Potato and Basil Purée (page 141)
1 stalk celery, diced	
1 medium Idaho potato, peeled and diced	*garnish* 4 large basil leaves
Salt to taste	

In a large pot, heat the olive oil over medium-high heat. When hot, add the diced vegetables. Season with salt, cover the pot, and let the vegetables cook for 5 minutes. Add water and Bouquet Garni. Let simmer for $1/2$ hour. Add peas and string beans and simmer 10 minutes longer. Discard Bouquet Garni.

Shape dumplings by molding spoonfuls of Potato and Basil Purée, using 2 tablespoons or soup spoons, into oval shapes. Put 3 dumplings into each of 4 soup plates. Bring the broth to a boil. Ladle broth over the dumplings, garnish with basil leaves, and serve immediately.

Tomato Consommé with Pea Pancakes

A true consommé is made from meat or poultry broth. This vegetable broth is easily made
sparkling clear by a classic technique. The eggshells and beaten whites absorb
any impurities in the broth. If you like, put a pea pancake in each soup plate
before filling with consommé—but serve right away so it doesn't get soggy.

SERVES 4

2 pounds tomatoes, quartered	Salt to taste
2 cups tomato juice	3 drops Tabasco
1 stalk celery with leaves, chopped	*garnish* 1 tomato, peeled, seeded, and diced
1 cup (lightly packed) basil leaves and stems	
5 egg whites, shells reserved	4 large basil leaves, cut into ribbons
	Pea Pancakes (recipe follows)

Combine tomatoes and tomato juice in a food processor or blender. Process until almost completely smooth. Pour mixture into a large pot and add the celery, basil leaves and stems, and the eggshells. Bring to a boil over medium-high heat. Reduce heat to medium and simmer for 10 minutes.

Whisk the egg whites lightly. Remove the tomato mixture from the heat and slowly whisk in the egg whites. Reduce heat to medium-low and add salt and Tabasco. Simmer for 10 minutes longer. Strain through a double layer of cheesecloth.

Serve the consommé either hot or cold and garnish with diced tomato and basil ribbons. Serve Pea Pancakes on the side.

Pea Pancakes

$1/2$ **pound fresh or frozen peas ($1^1/2$ cups)**
1 whole egg plus 1 egg yolk
Scant $1/2$ cup heavy cream
3 tablespoons all-purpose flour
5 tablespoons sweet butter
Salt and freshly ground pepper to taste

Cook the peas in boiling salted water until tender. Drain and set aside. Combine the peas, egg, yolk, cream, and flour in a food processor or blender and process until smooth. Brown 3 tablespoons butter and add to the egg mixture. Process to combine thoroughly and season with salt and pepper. Set aside until ready to use.

Melt the remaining 2 tablespoons butter in a medium sauté pan. Use about 1 tablespoon batter for each pancake. Cook on both sides until golden brown around the edges.

Oatmeal Pancakes

Serve these pancakes with applesauce or cranberry sauce and crisp bacon for breakfast. They are exquisite as an accompaniment to any fish. Try them with crème fraîche and smoked fish or caviar.

SERVES 4

Scant $^1/2$ cup milk	Salt and freshly ground pepper to taste
$1^1/3$ cups quick-cooking oats	$^1/4$ cup sweet butter
1 egg	3 tablespoons chopped shallots
1 tablespoon chopped parsley	(2 medium shallots)
1 tablespoon chopped cilantro	3 tablespoons chopped onion

Bring the milk to a boil and pour it over the oats. Let rest for 10 minutes. Stir in the egg, parsley, cilantro, salt, and pepper.

Melt 2 tablespoons butter in a small sauté pan over medium-high heat. Add the shallots and onion and cook until translucent. Add to the oatmeal batter.

Melt the remaining 2 tablespoons butter in a skillet. When hot, add the batter, 1 tablespoon per pancake. Cook until golden brown on both sides, about 30 seconds per side.

Skewered Polenta

Scant 1 cup milk	2 tablespoons freshly grated Parmesan cheese
2/3 cup yellow cornmeal (stoneground if possible)	Honey-Ginger Glazed Shallots (page 128)
1 egg yolk	

In a medium saucepan, bring the milk to a boil over medium-high heat. Slowly add the cornmeal and cook for 10 minutes, stirring constantly. Remove from heat and add the egg yolk and cheese. Pour into a loaf pan, 9 × 5 × 3 inches. Cover tightly and refrigerate until firm, about 10 minutes.

Cut into 1-inch cubes and thread 4 cubes onto each of 6 skewers. Grill until lightly marked or sauté in 2 tablespoons olive oil until golden brown. Serve with Honey-Ginger Glazed Shallots.

Corn Muffins

$1/2$ cup fresh or frozen corn

$1/2$ cup yellow cornmeal (stoneground if possible)

$1/2$ tablespoon baking powder

$1/2$ teaspoon baking soda

$1/2$ teaspoon sugar

$1/2$ teaspoon salt

$1/4$ cup all-purpose flour

2 tablespoons melted sweet butter

$1/4$ cup heavy cream

$1/2$ cup buttermilk

1 egg, separated

Heat the oven to 400°F.

Combine the corn and cornmeal in a food processor or blender and process for 30 seconds.

In a large mixing bowl, combine the dry ingredients. Add the corn mixture.

Combine the butter, cream, buttermilk, and egg yolk and mix thoroughly. Add to the dry ingredients. Beat until smooth.

Beat the egg white to stiff peaks. Fold into the batter.

Butter 6 cups of a regular-size muffin tin. Pour batter into each cup to fill three-fourths. Bake for 15 minutes.

Corn Pancakes

Two pancakes make an ample side dish serving to accompany roast duck, goose, turkey, or any bird.

SERVES 10

2/3 cup yellow cornmeal (stoneground if possible)	2 eggs
Scant 1 cup all-purpose flour	1 cup milk
Pinch sugar	3/4 cup fresh or frozen corn
	2 tablespoons sweet butter

In a large mixing bowl, combine the dry ingredients. Add eggs, milk, corn, and 1 1/2 tablespoons butter, melted and cooked until golden brown. Mix well.

Melt the remaining 1/2 tablespoon butter in a medium sauté pan. Use about 1 tablespoon batter for each pancake. Cook until golden brown on both sides, 30 seconds per side.

Spiced Rice

These cakes have a light crust but the rice inside is moist. This is a perfect complement to the soft-shell crabs on page 59 and many of the Asian dishes. I like to use basmati rice for this dish; the thin grains have extraordinary fragrance.

SERVES 4

1 cup long-grain rice	5 black peppercorns
2 1/2 cups water	Pinch of salt
1 stick cinnamon	2 tablespoons Clarified Butter (page 196)
1 bay leaf, broken into large pieces	or sweet butter
3 cloves	Large pinch saffron threads

In a medium saucepan, combine the rice, water, cinnamon, bay leaf, cloves, peppercorns, and salt. Cook over high heat for 10 minutes, until most of the water is absorbed.

Turn the rice into a strainer and rinse well under cold running water to remove excess starch. Discard the cinnamon and bay leaf pieces.

Heat the oven to 450°F.

Lightly butter the bottoms of four 3- to 4-ounce nonstick molds or one 8-inch nonstick pan. Scatter a few saffron threads over the bottom of the molds.

Pack rice into the molds no more than 1/2 to 3/4 inch deep.

Bake for 10 minutes. Unmold carefully. If a single large mold is used, cut into portions.

Rice Crackers

Savory and incredibly thin—these crackers are habit-forming and very easy to make.

SERVES 4

1 cup cooked risotto (page 158)

Heat the oven to 450°F.

Spread the risotto on nonstick baking sheets in a paper-thin layer. Bake until pale gold, about 5 minutes. Remove from the oven and cut into crackers, using a pizza wheel or sharp knife. Return to the oven and bake until golden brown and crisp, 3 to 5 minutes longer. Serve hot or cold.

Crisps of Risotto

We overcook the risotto for these crisps so the individual grains of rice seem to "melt" together.

MAKES 12 CRISPS

1/4 cup sweet butter	3 cups Mixed Vegetable Broth (page 68)
2 medium shallots, peeled and chopped (about 3 tablespoons)	1/4 cup freshly grated Parmesan
1/2 cup Arborio rice	Salt and freshly ground pepper to taste

Heat the oven to 450°F. Melt 2 tablespoons butter in an oven-proof pan over medium-high heat. Add the shallots and cook until translucent, about 1 minute.

Add the rice and sauté for 2 minutes, stirring constantly. Add the Mixed Vegetable Broth, cheese, salt, and pepper. Cover and bake for 20 minutes.

Remove from oven and spread mixture evenly in a jelly roll pan. Cover and refrigerate for 1 hour.

Shape into patties about 2 inches across and 1/2 inch thick. Melt the remaining 2 tablespoons butter in a large sauté pan over medium-high heat. When hot, add patties and cook until crisp and golden brown on both sides, about 2 minutes.

Onion Jam

Serve this rich jam with hot buttered toast, red meat, or boiled potatoes.
It will keep, tightly covered and refrigerated, for months.

SERVES 12

5 tablespoons sweet butter	1/2 cup grenadine
1 1/2 pounds onions, peeled and thinly sliced	1/2 cup red wine
3/4 cups sugar	1/2 cup red wine vinegar

Melt the butter in a large sauté pan over medium-high heat. Add the onions and cook until translucent, about 4 minutes, stirring occasionally. Add remaining ingredients and reduce heat to low. Cook for 1 1/2 hours, stirring occasionally, until all liquid has evaporated.

Fruits, Sorbets, Ice Creams, and Sweets

THE DESSERTS THAT FOLLOW WERE CREATED IN A SPIRIT OF LIGHTNESS AND SIMPLICITY. THEY CONTAIN NO FLOUR, AND MANY ARE MADE WITHOUT EGGS. AT RESTAURANT LAFAYETTE WE FOUND TRADITIONAL baked desserts were just too heavy after several courses. And, the idea of rapidly made desserts, refreshing and luscious with the flavors and textures of seasonal fruit, appealed to me as the perfect final note.

I'm including, too, a variety of rather different ice creams, sorbets, and granités (simple ices) that are wonderful on their own and especially nice served with the fruit desserts. Granités are very nice when served between courses, too. They can provide a refreshing break in the middle of longer menus, or when courses change from seafood to meat. They are so light that you can use them as you like.

Sautéed Rhubarb with Strawberries

SERVES 4

2 tablespoons sweet butter	18 large strawberries
4 cups peeled rhubarb, cut into $1/2$-inch chunks	Vanilla ice cream
2 tablespoons sugar	Vanilla Syrup (recipe follows)

Melt the butter in a large sauté pan over medium-high heat. Add the rhubarb, sprinkle with sugar, and sauté until tender, 4 to 5 minutes. Mash 12 strawberries and slice the remaining 6 in half. Arrange rhubarb in the center of each of 4 dessert plates. Add a scoop of vanilla ice cream, crushed berries, and top with sliced strawberries. Pour a little Vanilla Syrup around the outside of the plate.

Vanilla Syrup

$1/2$ large, moist vanilla bean
$1/4$ cup Simple Syrup (page 196)

Slice the vanilla bean in half lengthwise. Scrape the vanilla grains into a small cup and mix with Simple Syrup. Reserve the bean for another use.

Tropical Medley

1 tablespoon sweet butter	1 medium passion fruit
1/2 medium pineapple, peeled and cut into large dice	1/2 cup packed dark brown sugar
1 medium mango, peeled and cut into large dice	3/4 cup dark rum
1 medium red papaya, peeled, seeded, and cut into large dice	Lemongrass Sorbet (page 176)

Melt the butter in a medium sauté pan over medium-high heat. Add pineapple and sauté for 1 minute. Add the mango and the papaya and sauté until hot. Cut the passion fruit in half and scrape the pulp and seeds into the pan. Sprinkle with sugar and deglaze the pan with the rum. Simmer for 2 minutes over medium heat to reduce liquid slightly. Transfer to a large plate and refrigerate until fruit has cooled to room temperature. To serve, spoon 1/2 cup of fruit onto each serving plate. Serve with Lemongrass Sorbet.

Orange Blossom Pots de Crème

SERVES 8

1 quart plus 1 cup heavy cream	1/2 cup sugar
2 tablespoons orange blossom (orange flower) water	*garnish* Rose Petal Jam (recipe follows)
12 egg yolks	2 tablespoons chopped pistachios

Heat the oven to 250°F.

In a large saucepan, combine the cream and orange blossom water over medium-high heat. Bring to a boil and immediately remove from heat. Let sit at room temperature for 1/2 hour. Whisk egg yolks and sugar together until light and fluffy. Bring the cream mixture back to a boil and pour in a thin stream into the yolks, whisking constantly. Strain the mixture and ladle into eight 3- to 4-ounce ramekins. Place ramekins in a deep baking pan. Pour hot water into the pan to reach halfway up the ramekins. Bake for 30 to 40 minutes, until a knife inserted in the center comes out clean. Let cool to room temperature. Cover tightly and refrigerate for 2 hours before serving. Garnish each pot de crème with a dollop of Rose Petal Jam and a sprinkling of pistachios.

Rose Petal Jam

1/2 cup Simple Syrup (page 196)
1 cup pink rose petals (unsprayed)
1 tablespoon rose water
1 teaspoon fresh lemon juice

In a small saucepan, bring the Simple Syrup to a simmer over low heat. Add the rose petals, rose water, and lemon juice. Cook, stirring occasionally, until the petals are wilted and syrup is thick, about 10 minutes.

Cold Kiwi Soup

When a food mill is used to purée the kiwis, the resulting color is a brilliant green. A food processor or blender can be used, but it will liquify the fruit to a more pastel purée.

Scant 1 cup dry white wine	2 tablespoons fresh lemon juice
3 tablespoons honey	1/4 cup sugar
11 kiwis	20 large strawberries, sliced in half
1 medium apple (Cortland, Granny Smith, or other tart apple)	

In a nonreactive saucepan, combine the wine and honey over medium-high heat. Bring to a boil, remove from heat, and let cool to room temperature. Peel 8 kiwis, quarter them, and remove the white pith. Put through the medium disc of a food mill and mix the purée with the wine syrup. Cover tightly and refrigerate at least 3 hours.

Peel remaining kiwis and cut into eighths. Peel and dice the apple. Toss first in the lemon juice, then sugar. Arrange kiwi and strawberry slices around the inside of each of 4 soup plates. Ladle in cold kiwi mixture over the fruit and garnish with a few pieces of sugared apple.

Apricot Gratin with
Almond Milk Ice Cream

SERVES 4

1 cup finely ground almonds	4 teaspoons amaretto
2 tablespoons plus 4 teaspoons sweet butter	8 apricots, halved and pitted
4 teaspoons sugar	$1/2$ cup dry white wine
	Almond Milk Ice Cream (page 171)

Heat the oven to 450°F.

Mix the ground almonds, 4 teaspoons butter, sugar, and amaretto to a paste. Fill the apricot halves with the mixture.

Place the stuffed apricots in a broiler-proof pan. Pour the wine around them and add the remaining 2 tablespoons butter. Bake for 10 minutes. Remove from the oven and place under a preheated broiler, about 6 inches from the heat, to glaze the almond filling. Remove apricots to serving plates. Reduce the cooking liquid to a syrup. Serve the apricots with Almond Milk Ice Cream and some of the syrup.

Litchis with Bitter Almond Pancakes

Fresh litchis are admittedly a luxury. If they are not to be found, substitute canned litchis;
they will not need to be cooked.

SERVES 4

24 fresh litchis, peeled and rinsed	2 tablespoons fresh lemon juice
1 cup sugar	Bitter Almond Pancakes (recipe follows)
4 cups water	

In a large saucepan, combine the litchis, sugar, water, and lemon juice over medium heat. Poach the litchis until they are tender, about 10 minutes.

Let cool in the poaching liquid. When cooled to room temperature, cover tightly and refrigerate until cold.

Serve 6 litchis per person with some of the poaching liquid and Bitter Almond Pancakes on the side.

Bitter Almond Pancakes

1 cup finely ground almonds
1 egg
1 egg yolk
3/4 cup heavy cream
1 tablespoon sugar
4 tablespoons sweet butter, cooked until golden brown and cooled
2 tablespoons almond extract

Heat the oven to 350°F.

Mix all ingredients to a smooth batter. Spoon onto a nonstick baking sheet, using 1 teaspoon batter for each pancake. Bake for 10 minutes. Turn the pancakes over and bake for 2 minutes longer. Let cool slightly on the baking sheet.

Winter Compote

Scant 1/2 cup each of the following unsweetened, dried fruits[*]: raisins, currants, cherries, blueberries, cranberries, strawberries, dates, pears, peaches, figs, and apricots

Grated zest of 1 medium orange

2 tablespoons sugar

1 tablespoon honey

2 tablespoons chopped fresh ginger

1 moist vanilla bean, halved lengthwise and the grains loosened

1 stick cinnamon

1 tablespoon fresh lemon juice

2 cups dry red wine

Bitter Cocoa Sorbet (page 177)

Cut the larger dried fruits into strips; keep small ones whole.

In a medium nonreactive saucepan, combine the remaining ingredients except the sorbet over medium-high heat. Bring to a boil, add the fruits, and simmer for 20 minutes. Remove vanilla bean and cinnamon stick. Serve with Bitter Cocoa Sorbet.

[*]*Use as great a variety of dried fruits as you can find—the more, the better.*

Apple Compote with Rosemary

4 medium Granny Smith apples
3/4 cup sliced almonds
1 tablespoon sweet butter
2 tablespoons plus 2 teaspoons honey

1/4 teaspoon fresh rosemary leaves or 1/8
teaspoon dried rosemary
1 cup plus 2 tablespoons water
4 apricots, peeled and pitted
2 tablespoons Simple Syrup (page 196)

Peel the apples and cut into small dice. Put in a medium saucepan with the almonds, butter, honey, rosemary, and 1/2 cup water. Cover and cook over medium-low heat until liquid evaporates. Uncover and cook until apples caramelize, about 5 minutes longer. Add 1/2 cup water and cook until it evaporates. Set aside and keep warm.

Combine the apricots, 2 tablespoons water, and Simple Syrup in a blender. Blend until smooth. Serve with the compote.

Roast Figs with Port Wine

SERVES 4

16 medium figs	1 stick cinnamon
2 teaspoons sweet butter	1 teaspoon fresh lemon juice
3/4 cup port wine	Three-Spice Ice Cream (page 174)
3/4 cup dry red wine	

Heat the oven to 450°F.

Slash each fig 2 or 3 times. Melt the butter in an oven-proof pan over medium-high heat and add the figs. Cook for 1 minute. Deglaze the pan with port and red wine, and add the cinnamon stick. Put the pan in the oven and roast for 5 minutes.

Remove the figs. Reduce the cooking liquid on top of the stove to a syrup and add the lemon juice. Arrange the figs in small bowls around scoops of Three-Spice Ice Cream with some of the sauce spooned on top.

Hot Cherries with Honey Kirsch

SERVES 4

4 tablespoons honey	2 teaspoons kirsch
4 cups pitted fresh sweet cherries	Pistachio Ice Cream (page 172)
2 teaspoons sweet butter	
	garnish 4 teaspoons chopped pistachios

In a medium sauté pan, cook the honey over medium-high heat until it caramelizes, about 2 minutes. Add the cherries and stir to coat well. Add the butter and stir until it melts. Deglaze the pan with kirsch and cook for 2 minutes longer.

Put a scoop of Pistachio Ice Cream in each of 4 serving dishes. Pour the cherries and sauce over the ice cream and sprinkle with chopped pistachios.

Almond Milk Ice Cream

MAKES ABOUT 6 CUPS

2 cups milk	8 egg whites
2 cups heavy cream	$2/3$ cup sugar
1 moist vanilla bean	1 cup finely ground almonds

Combine milk and cream. Cut the vanilla bean in half lengthwise and, with the point of a knife, scrape the tiny seeds into the cream mixture. Add the bean and let infuse for $1/2$ hour.

In a mixing bowl, combine the egg whites and sugar. Bring the cream mixture to a boil. Slowly pour about one-third of the cream mixture over the egg whites and sugar, whisking vigorously. Pour the mixture into the saucepan, bring to a boil, and boil for 1 minute, stirring constantly with a wooden spoon. Pour the mixture into a mixing bowl and stir in the ground almonds. Let cool to room temperature, then strain. Process in an ice cream maker according to the manufacturer's instructions.

Pistachio Ice Cream

1^1/2 cups milk	8 egg yolks
1^1/2 cups heavy cream	^{1}/2 cup sugar
1^1/2 cups pistachios	

In a medium saucepan, combine the milk, cream, and pistachios. Bring to a boil, remove from the heat, and let infuse for 1 hour.

Pour the mixture into a food processor or blender. Process until nuts are finely chopped; return the mixture to the saucepan. Whisk the egg yolks and sugar until light and fluffy. Bring the pistachio cream to a boil. Pour about one-third of the pistachio cream over the yolks while beating vigorously. Pour the mixture back into the saucepan. Cook over very low heat, stirring constantly with a wooden spoon, until thick enough to coat the spoon. Remove from heat and strain into a medium mixing bowl. Set the bowl into a larger bowl of ice water and whisk until cool. (Or cover and refrigerate until cool.) Process in an ice cream maker according to the manufacturer's instructions.

Ginger Ice Cream

MAKES ABOUT 5 CUPS

1 cup coarsely chopped plus 2 tablespoons finely chopped fresh ginger	1 1/2 cups heavy cream
1 1/2 cups milk	8 egg yolks
	1/2 cup sugar

Put the coarsely chopped ginger in a small saucepan with just enough water to cover. Boil for 5 minutes. Drain the ginger and put it in a medium saucepan with the milk and cream. Bring to a boil; let infuse for 1 hour.

Whisk the yolks and sugar until light and fluffy. Bring the ginger cream to a boil. Pour about one-third of the ginger cream over the yolks while beating vigorously. Pour the mixture back into the saucepan. Cook over very low heat, stirring constantly with a wooden spoon, until thick enough to coat the spoon. Remove from heat and strain into a medium mixing bowl. Set the bowl into a larger bowl of ice water. (Or cover and refrigerate until cool.) Add finely chopped ginger and process in an ice cream maker according to the manufacturer's instructions.

Three-Spice Ice Cream

1^1/$_2$ cups milk	2 teaspoons ground allspice
1^1/$_2$ cups heavy cream	8 egg yolks
^{1}/$_4$ cup crushed star anise or fennel seed	^{1}/$_2$ cup sugar
3 sticks cinnamon	^{1}/$_2$ teaspoon finely chopped fresh ginger

In a medium saucepan, combine the milk, cream, and spices. Bring to a boil and let infuse for 1 hour.

Strain into a clean saucepan. Whisk the yolks and sugar until light and fluffy. Bring the spice cream to a boil. Pour about one-third of the spice cream over the yolks while beating vigorously. Pour the mixture back into the saucepan. Cook over very low heat, stirring constantly with a wooden spoon, until thick enough to coat the spoon. Remove from heat and strain into a medium mixing bowl. Set the bowl into a larger bowl of ice water. (Or cover and refrigerate until cool.) Add finely chopped ginger and process in an ice cream maker according to the manufacturer's instructions.

Cardamom Ice Cream

1 1/2 cups milk	Grated zest of 1 small orange
1 1/2 cups heavy cream	8 egg yolks
2 tablespoons crushed green cardamom seeds	1/2 cup sugar

In a medium saucepan, combine the milk, cream, cardamom seeds, and orange zest. Bring to a boil and let infuse for 1 hour.

Strain into a clean saucepan. Whisk the yolks and sugar until light and fluffy. Bring the cream mixture to a boil. Pour about one-third of the cream mixture over the yolks while beating vigorously. Pour the mixture back into the saucepan. Cook over very low heat, stirring constantly with a wooden spoon, until thick enough to coat the spoon. Remove from heat and strain into a medium mixing bowl. Set the bowl into a larger bowl of ice water. (Or cover and refrigerate until cool.) Process in an ice cream maker according to the manufacturer's instructions.

Lemongrass Sorbet

2 cups fresh lemon juice	$2/3$ cup sugar
2 cups dry white wine	7 stalks lemongrass, coarsely chopped
$1/2$ cup light corn syrup	

In a medium nonreactive saucepan, combine all ingredients. Bring to a boil and let infuse for 1 hour. Strain the liquid and process in an ice cream maker according to manufacturer's instructions.

Bitter Cocoa Sorbet

1 3/4 cups water	1/2 cup good-quality cocoa powder
1/2 cup sugar	3 1/2 ounces good-quality unsweetened chocolate, melted
Grated zest of 1 medium orange	

In a medium saucepan, combine the water, sugar, and zest. Bring to a boil and whisk in the cocoa powder and chocolate. When the mixture returns to a boil, remove from heat and strain into a medium mixing bowl. Set the bowl into a larger bowl of ice water. (Or cover and refrigerate until cool.) Process in an ice cream maker according to the manufacturer's instructions.

Tamarillo Sorbet

MAKES ABOUT 5 CUPS

9 tamarillos, peeled and coarsely chopped
1³/₄ cups sugar

3 cups dry white wine

In a medium nonreactive saucepan, combine all ingredients. Bring to a boil and simmer for 4 minutes. Transfer to a food processor or blender and process until smooth. Strain and let cool. Process in an ice cream maker according to the manufacturer's instructions.

A WORD ABOUT GRANITÉS

Granités are made differently than sorbets. Where a sorbet is smooth, a proper granité is made up of larger icy particles. Depending on the composition of a particular granité (and how it is scraped from its freezing tray), a granité can be served as an icy mound of delicate flakes or chunky grains.

Cranberry-Champagne Granité

1 cup cranberry juice	1 cup brut champagne
2 tablespoons Simple Syrup (page 196)	

Combine all ingredients. Pour into a 13 × 9-inch baking pan and freeze for 4 hours.

Remove from the freezer. Scrape the surface of the ice with a spoon or fork into large, flaky crystals.

Grapefruit-Campari Granité

2 cups fresh grapefruit juice	2 tablespoons Campari
1/4 cup Simple Syrup (page 196)	

Combine all ingredients. Pour into a 13 × 9-inch baking pan and freeze for 4 hours.

Remove from the freezer. Scrape the surface of the ice with a spoon or fork into large, flaky crystals.

Tequila-Lime Granité

MAKES ABOUT 2 1/4 CUPS

1 1/4 cups fresh lime juice	1/4 cup Simple Syrup (page 196)
1/4 cup water	1/2 cup tequila

Combine all ingredients. Pour into a 13 × 9-inch baking pan and freeze for 4 hours.

Remove from the freezer. Scrape the surface of the ice with a spoon or fork into large, flaky crystals.

Orange-Lillet Granité

2 cups fresh orange juice
1/4 cup Simple Syrup (page 196)

1/2 cup light Lillet

Combine all ingredients. Pour into a 13 × 9-inch baking pan and freeze for 4 hours.

Remove from the freezer. Scrape the surface of the ice with a spoon or fork into large, flaky crystals.

Espresso-Lemon Granité

MAKES ABOUT 2 1/2 CUPS

1 1/4 cups decaffeinated espresso
1/4 cup Tia Maria or similar coffee-
    flavored liqueur

1/4 cup Simple Syrup (page 196)
3/4 cup water
1 tablespoon grated lemon zest

Combine all ingredients. Pour into a 13 × 9-inch baking pan and freeze for 4 hours.

Remove from the freezer. Scrape the surface of the ice with a spoon or fork into large, flaky crystals.

An American Accent

YOU CAN SEE FROM THE RECIPES THAT FOLLOW THAT I'VE BEEN EXPERI-
MENTING A BIT WITH AMERICAN COOKING. I REALLY LIKE AMERICAN
FOOD, SOMETIMES CRAVE IT.

Lots of us prefer straightforward, simply flavored food. It has been my
experience that even those who are dubious about "fancy" food (including
children who turn up their noses at most "grown-up" food) positively devour
the Tuna Sandwich (page 187) and the Lamb Burger (page 189). The Shrimp
Cocktail (page 186) is unbelievably easy for all its unusual effect—perfect for
entertaining—and the Tomato Salad (page 190) is for anyone who ever felt
they couldn't get too much of a good thing.

Americans excel at many things, and one of these is barbecue. I
wouldn't presume to tell an American how to barbecue, but I'd like to sug-
gest that flavored oils make exceptional marinades. Marinate the foods that
follow in the suggested oils, for starters, but feel free to try other flavored
oils, too. Simply prepare the oil of your choice. Marinate the meat or seafood
in the refrigerator overnight (or at least 6 hours) in enough oil to half cover
it. Turn it several times if possible while it marinates.

Ribs	**Paprika Oil**
Steak	**all Mild Herb Oils; Garlic, Mustard, and Rosemary Oils**
Hamburger	**all Mild Herb Oils; Cumin and Wasabi Oils**
Chicken	**Curry, Ginger, Orange-Basil, and Tarragon Oils**
Fish	**all Herb Oils; Fennel, Lobster, Saffron, and Shrimp Oils**
Shrimp	**Cardamom, Curry, Ginger, Lobster, Pineapple-Cilantro, and Shrimp Oils**

American Iced Shrimp Cocktail

SERVES 4

2 cups fresh (strained) or canned tomato juice	Salt and freshly ground pepper to taste
Pinch of celery salt	1 pound jumbo shrimp, peeled and deveined
Dash of Tabasco	Small leaves of arugula or basil
2 tablespoons prepared horseradish	

Thoroughly combine all ingredients except the shrimp and arugula. Pour into a flat container to a depth of $1/2$ inch. Freeze until firm.

In a wok or steamer, steam the shrimp for 3 minutes (10 minutes for shrimp wrapped in plastic wrap, if following the technique on page 93). Let shrimp rest 1 minute. Divide the shrimp among 4 serving plates.

Break the tomato ice into pieces and arrange $1/4$ cup next to the shrimp on each plate. Decorate with arugula leaves.

Tuna Sandwich

I love this sandwich cooked quickly, 1 minute per side. Use ordinary white bread as you would for any sandwich. You may want to try this with salmon instead of tuna.

SERVES 1

2 slices white sandwich bread, crusts trimmed	1 egg yolk beaten with 1 tablespoon water
3-ounce slice fresh tuna (1 inch thick)	Salt and freshly ground pepper to taste
	2 tablespoons extra virgin olive oil

With a rolling pin, flatten each slice of bread until thin.

Trim the tuna so it will fit neatly on one slice of bread, leaving a $1/4$-inch border around the tuna.

Brush one slice of bread, right to the edges, with egg yolk. Place the tuna in the center and season lightly with salt and pepper.

Cover with the other slice of bread. Press the edges together to make a package; the egg will help seal it.

In a small sauté pan, heat the olive oil until hot. Add the sandwich and cook over medium-high heat until golden brown on both sides, about 1 minute per side for rare tuna, 2 minutes per side for medium.

Remove from the pan and lightly pat dry with paper toweling to remove excess oil. Cut into quarters and serve immediately.

Potato Club Sandwich

This "sandwich" is built using crisp fried potatoes in place of bread. You can, of course, use any combination of meats for this sandwich. You can play with another American favorite in similar fashion, layering scrambled eggs and bacon with potato lattices. Enjoy!

SERVES 1

1 large Idaho potato, peeled	Extra virgin olive oil
1 cup melted sweet butter or peanut oil	Balsamic vinegar
Salt to taste	2 or 3 thin slices ham
3 or 4 leaves of salad greens	2 or 3 thin slices turkey
2 thin slices tomato	3 or 4 thin slices avocado

Heat the oven to 450°F.

Slice the potato lengthwise, no more than 1/16 inch thick. Use a mandoline if you have one. You want very thin, oval slices. Cut each slice into 4 thin rectangles. (A large potato will yield about 40 rectangular strips.)

Toss the strips in butter and drain any excess. Arrange 8 strips with space between them in a grid on a nonstick baking sheet. (It will look like a large tic-tac-toe pattern.) Make 4 potato grids.

Bake until golden brown, 10 to 15 minutes. Gently turn over and bake until brown, about 5 minutes longer. Lightly salt.

To assemble the sandwich, place 1 potato grid on a serving plate. Cover with a few lettuce leaves and tomato slices lightly coated with a little olive oil and vinegar. Top with a potato grid. Cover with ham and turkey and top with another potato grid. Top with the remaining lettuce, avocado, and a final potato grid. Drizzle some olive oil and vinegar around the plate. Serve with a sprig of fresh herb through the top.

Lamb Burger with Goat Cheese

I made this dish on the grill this summer, using goat.

With freshly made shoestring potatoes, it was a great treat.

SERVES 4

1 1/2 pounds ground lamb or baby goat	2 tablespoons chopped cilantro
Pinch cayenne pepper	1/4 cup soft white goat cheese, such as Montrachet
2 pinches ground cinnamon	
Salt and freshly ground pepper to taste	Sauce (recipe follows)

Combine the lamb, cayenne pepper, cinnamon, salt, and pepper. Shape into 4 patties. Combine the cilantro and cheese. Make a pocket in the center of each patty and stuff with the cheese mixture. Cover the cheese completely with meat.

Sauté over medium-high heat or grill for 7 to 10 minutes (depending on how you like your burger cooked).

Sauce

1 cup plain goat or cow's milk yogurt
1 tablespoon cumin seeds
1/2 cup chopped, seeded cucumber
Pinch each of salt and cayenne pepper

Combine all ingredients and refrigerate until needed.

Tomato Salad with Tomato Water

Tomato salad is a wonderful American dish. Remember that tomatoes are best in the summertime, and any tomato salad is only as good as the tomatoes that go into it. Serve a little glass of the richly flavored Tomato Water with the salad, or with the Tomato and Basil Tart (page 101). To each cup of Tomato Water, add a few drops of vodka and Tabasco sauce for a very light Bloody Mary.

SERVES 4, WITH 1 1/2 TO 2 CUPS TOMATO WATER

4 ripe beefsteak or other large, flavorful tomatoes	1/2 cup extra virgin olive oil
Salt and freshly ground pepper to taste	1 tablespoon boiling water
1/4 cup vinegar	1 teaspoon each chopped basil, mint, and parsley

Blanch the tomatoes in boiling water for 30 seconds. Immediately refresh under cold running water for 10 seconds. Remove skins. Slice the tomatoes 1/2 inch thick and reserve the juice. Season tomatoes with salt and pepper.

Put the tomatoes and their juice in a bag made from 4 layers of cheesecloth. Suspend the bag over a large bowl in the refrigerator and allow "water" to drip for 4 hours. Keep Tomato Water refrigerated until ready to use.

Combine the vinegar, olive oil, and boiling water in a blender. Blend until emulsified. Add basil, mint, and parsley.

Arrange the tomato slices on a large serving plate and dress with vinaigrette.

Thirty-Minute Menus and Menus for Special Occasions

AT THE END OF A BUSY DAY OR EVEN ON THE WEEKEND, MANY OF US DON'T WANT TO BOTHER COOKING COMPLICATED MEALS THAT TAKE A GREAT DEAL OF TIME TO PREPARE. WITH ONLY A LITTLE PRACTICE, THE FOLLOWING MENUS may be prepared in less than 30 minutes.

When you have prepared any of the vinaigrettes, flavored oils, or broths in advance, you'll save even more time. Remember, too, that you can make the fillings for the phyllo dishes in the morning or even a day ahead.

I haven't suggested desserts for these menus. Any of the ice creams, sorbets, or granités would be very nice. In addition, the following desserts are very quick to prepare:

**Sautéed Rhubarb
with Strawberries**

Tropical Medley

Cold Kiwi Soup

**Apple Compote
with Rosemary**

Roast Figs with Port Wine

Hot Cherries with Honey Kirsch

The menus that follow are intended to help you put a marvelous dinner on the table with a minimum of time and fuss.

Of course you can combine any of the rapidly prepared appetizers with the sautéed or steamed dishes (pages 86 to 94) for an equally rapid meal. If I am preparing one course with a flavored oil, I like to use a broth, vinaigrette, or juice in another course, because I enjoy the variety. You might prefer all-vinaigrette or all-juice menus, playing the flavors against each other.

Asparagus Salad
Monkfish with Mushroom Syrup

Cold Cucumber Soup with Dill Oil
Lamb in a Potato Crust

Shrimp Salad with Curry Oil
Fillet of Red Snapper with Citrus Vinaigrette

Poached Foie Gras with Fennel
and Caramel Pepper
Salmon Cabbage with Juniper Vinaigrette

Veal in Rice Paper
Whiting with Endive Broth

Tomato and Basil Tart
Sea Scallops with Zucchini Juice

Foie Gras with Ginger and Mango
Shrimp with Spicy Carrot Juice

Rabbit Sausage with Mustard Oil
Lobster with Asparagus Juice

Thai Shrimp Cakes
Chicken in Pineapple Juice

Alsatian Tart
Halibut with Truffle and Yellow Bell Pepper Oil

Shrimp and Chicken in Lemon Grass Broth
Red Snapper with Potato Flakes and Tomato Oil

Cheese Gallette with Pecans
Cod Cakes with Orange-Basil Oil

Tempura with Cabbage Salad and Cinnamon Oil
Watercress Broth with Yellow Pike

Salmon Leaves with Rosemary Oil
Veal with Celery Juice and Roquefort

Lobster Strudel or Shrimp,
Tomato, and Cilantro Tart
Lacquered Quail with Sesame Seeds

Chanterelle and Spinach Salad
Chicken with Lime and Honey

Goat Cheese with Watercress Oil
Tuna Sandwich

American Iced Shrimp Cocktail
Lamb Burger with Goat Cheese

Shrimp in a Spiced Orange and Sauternes Broth
Marinated Lemon Chicken with Fennel Oil

Goat Cheese Bricks with Endive Salad
Watercress Broth with Yellow Pike

Rice Paper Sushi
Soft-Shell Crabs with Carrot-Cinnamon Oil

Tuna Tartare with Gaufrette Potatoes
Cod with Pink Radish Juice

Tuna Tartare with Assorted Chips and Oils
Potato Club Sandwich

MENUS FOR SPECIAL OCCASIONS

Spring

Shrimp in Spicy Carrot Juice
Lamb in a Potato Crust
Sautéed Rhubarb with Strawberries

Summer

Sea Scallops with Zucchini Juice
Salmon in a Shiitake Shell
Cold Kiwi Soup

Fall

Alsatian Tart
*Monkfish Medallions with
Mushroom Syrup*
Apple Compote with Rosemary

Winter

Sweetbreads with Yellow Potato Salad
Halibut with Truffle and Yellow Bell Pepper Oil
Winter Compote with Bitter Cocoa Sorbet

Menu Poissons

Tuna Tartare with Gaufrette Potatoes
Watercress Broth with Yellow Pike
Lobster with Parsnip Purée
Orange Blossom Pots de Cre[ag]me

Menu de Fêtes

Marble of Foie Gras
Sea Scallops in Leek "Juice"
Lamb in a Potato Crust
*Hot Cherries with
Honey Kirsch*

Menu Asiatique

Eggs with Oysters
Thai Shrimp Cakes
*Lacquered Quail with
Sesame Seeds*
*Litchis with Bitter Almond
Pancakes*

Pantry Basics and Uncommon Garnishes

WITH THESE FEW BASIC INGREDIENTS ON HAND, YOU CAN BE PREPARED FOR JUST ABOUT ANY RECIPE THAT APPEALS TO YOU. I'VE COME TO THINK OF THE FLAVORED OILS, VINAIGRETTES, JUICES, AND BROTHS AS basics; at least, that is how I use them now. But here is a handful of somewhat less glamorous basics. Two of them take refrigerator staples and make them into versatile sauces. The others keep well. Some of my recipes call for them, and you'll find you will use them on your own, too.

PANTRY BASICS

Here are two very fast and flavorful recipes that perfectly complement meat and fish. The sauces are based on two American favorites: mustard and ketchup.

MUSTARD WINE SAUCE

In a small nonreactive saucepan, bring $1/2$ cup dry white wine to a boil. Boil for 3 minutes.

Add 1 tablespoon Dijon mustard, 2 tablespoons minced parsley or chives, and salt and freshly ground pepper to taste. Mix well. Bring to a boil and serve.

KETCHUP SAUCE

In a small saucepan, melt 2 tablespoons sweet butter over medium heat and cook until golden brown.

Add 1 tablespoon ketchup, 3 tablespoons sherry vinegar, and 1 tablespoon each of diced apple, capers, diced tomato, and minced parsley. Add salt and freshly ground pepper to taste, and mix well. Bring to a boil and serve.

note   *As good as this is with steak, chicken, and pork chops, it is superb with sautéed or steamed skate, black bass, halibut, and other strongly flavored fish.*

BOUQUET GARNI

This is a small bundle of herbs that, immersed in a liquid, flavors while it cooks. Remember to remove the Bouquet Garni before serving. You can add any herbs you like.

1/4 cup chopped leek (green part only)
1 bay leaf
Several sprigs thyme
Several sprigs parsley

Combine the herbs on a 4-inch square of triple-thickness cheesecloth. Tie them up in the cheesecloth with kitchen string to make a secure bundle.

CLARIFIED BUTTER

Clarifying butter is a process that removes the milk solids, leaving a clear, deep yellow butter that is less apt to burn at higher temperatures.

MAKES 3/4 CUP

1 cup sweet butter

Melt the butter in the top of a double boiler set over—not touching—boiling water. When the butter has melted completely, remove the top pan and let stand for 10 minutes. Skim as much of the white foam from the surface as possible. Let stand at room temperature 30 minutes longer.

Carefully pour the clear yellow butter into a clean container, leaving the milky solids behind. Or, strain the liquid through several layers of cheesecloth, rinsed in cool water and thoroughly wrung out, into a clean container. Store in the refrigerator, tightly covered, up to 2 months.

SIMPLE SYRUP

Ordinary granulated sugar sometimes doesn't dissolve completely. Use Simple Syrup as a substitute for granulated sugar. It ensures smooth (not grainy) results without sugar crystals.

MAKES 3 CUPS

2 cups water
2 cups sugar

Combine ingredients in a saucepan over medium heat. Bring to a boil, remove from heat, and let cool. Pour into a clean glass jar. Store tightly covered in a kitchen cupboard. There is no need to refrigerate.

UNCOMMON GARNISHES

I always appreciate the little finishing touches that make a plate look truly dressed. But I prefer garnishes that add something more than visual amusement. Many of the flavored oils, of course, can be great fun—they are beautiful in themselves—and they taste wonderful. Here are two more ways to garnish: Fried Vegetable Accents, and a lovely old Provençal recipe for Sautéed Panisses.

FRIED VEGETABLE ACCENTS

When deep-fat fried, thinly sliced vegetables become crisp and yet keep both their color and flavor. You can prepare them hours in advance if you like, and they go a long way; just a few to a plate should be enough.

Celery Leaves	Celeriac Chips
Beet Chips	Celery Julienne
Carrot Julienne	Asparagus Peelings
Lotus Root Chips	Mushroom Chips
Leek Julienne	Eggplant Julienne
Leek/Beet/Zucchini/ Lotus Root/Eggplant or Carrot Baskets	

Pat any moist vegetables dry with paper toweling.

Fry chips and juliennes at 350° to 375°F in 2 inches of vegetable oil, baskets in oil to cover.

Remove from the oil with a slotted spoon. The vegetables will be somewhat fragile and will become more crisp after being removed from the oil. Let cool slightly, then test for crispness. If not crisp enough, return them to the pot for a few seconds longer.

After frying, drain the vegetables on paper toweling and lightly salt.

Celery Leaves	Remove leaves from celery. Fry until crisp, about 10 seconds.
Celeriac Chips	Peel the celeriac root and slice paper thin. Fry until crisp, about 30 seconds. Season with celery salt.
Beet Chips	Peel the beet and slice paper thin. Set on paper toweling and let dry for 1/2 hour. Lightly dust with flour, and shake off any excess. Fry until crisp, 15 to 20 seconds.
Celery Julienne	Use very fine julienne. Lightly dust with flour and shake off any excess. Fry until crisp, about 10 seconds. Season with celery salt.
Carrot Julienne	Use very fine julienne. Lightly dust with flour and shake off any excess. Fry until crisp, about 10 seconds.
Asparagus Peelings	With a vegetable peeler, thinly peel until all of the spear is used. Fry until crisp, about 10 seconds.
Lotus Root Chips	Peel the lotus root and slice paper thin. Fry until crisp, about 15 seconds.

Mushroom Chips	Trim and thinly slice mushrooms. Fry until crisp, about 15 seconds.
Leek Julienne	Use very fine julienne. Lightly dust with flour and shake off any excess. Fry until crisp, about 10 seconds.
Eggplant Julienne	Use very fine julienne. Lightly dust with flour and shake off any excess. Fry until crisp, about 10 seconds.
Leek/Beet/Zucchini/ Lotus Root/Eggplant or Carrot Baskets	Use very fine julienne. Lightly dust with flour and shake off any excess. Place in a small, round frying basket so as to cover the inside of the basket. Place a second basket over the vegetables, holding them in place. Fry until crisp, about 1 minute. Gently remove from the frying basket.

SAUTEED PANISSES

This Provençal specialty is something between a garnish and a side dish. Every piece is crunchy on the outside, creamy inside. Be sure not to make it more than $1/2$ inch thick. Use canapé or cookie cutters to cut it out, or cut into shapes freehand.

SERVES 4

1 quart milk
2 tablespoons sweet butter
Scant 2 cups chickpea flour
Salt and freshly ground pepper to taste
$1/2$ cup extra virgin olive oil

In a medium saucepan, bring the milk and butter to boil over medium-high heat. Slowly add the chickpea flour, whisking constantly. Simmer, stirring constantly, for 5 minutes. Mixture should be thick and free of lumps. Season with salt and pepper. Pour into a well-buttered 9-inch square pan. Refrigerate until set, about 10 minutes.

Cut into desired shapes. In a large sauté pan, heat the olive oil until hot. Add the pieces and cook until golden brown on all sides, about 2 minutes.

Cross-Reference of Juices, Vinaigrettes, Oils, and Broths

JUICES

Asparagus	Lobster with Asparagus Juice
Beet	Beet-Ginger Oil
	Black Bass with Beet Juice and Caviar
Bell Pepper	Bell Pepper Oil
Broccoli	Crab Cakes with Broccoli Juice
Carrot	Carrot-Cinnamon Oil
	Shrimp in Spicy Carrot Juice
	Spicy Carrot Juice
Celery	Veal with Celery Juice and Roquefort Cheese
	Yellow Pike with Celery Juice
Chive	Chive Oil
Dill	Dill Oil
Fennel	Smoked Salmon Custard with Fennel Juice
Leek	Sea Scallops in Leek Juice
Pineapple	Chicken in Pineapple Juice
Tomato	Tomato Oil
Radish	Cod with Pink Radish Juice
Watercress	Watercress Oil
Zucchini	Lamb Cannelloni with Zucchini Juice
	Sea Scallops with Zucchini Juice
	Zucchini Juice with Thyme

VINAIGRETTES

Basil
Beef on a String with Basil Vinaigrette
Salad of Crayfish, Zucchini, and Tomato

Caviar
Buckwheat Pasta with Black Bass and Caviar

Citrus
Salmon in Rice Paper with Citrus Vinaigrette

Ginger
Cold Sea Urchin Soufflé
Lobster Couscous
Sweetbread Fritters with Ginger Vinaigrette

Hazelnut
Broccoli Mousse with Truffle Vinaigrette
Chanterelle and Spinach Salad
Sweetbreads with Yellow Potato Salad
Wild Mushroom Gâteau

Juniper
Salmon Cabbage with Juniper Vinaigrette

Lobster
Open Ravioli with Shrimp
Skate Wings with Artichokes

Peanut
Broccoli Mousse with Truffle Vinaigrette
Foie Gras with Fried Leeks
Squab and Lentil Salad

Shrimp
Open Ravioli with Shrimp
Skate Wings with Artichokes

Soy and Ginger
Asparagus Salad
Duck Bricks
Steamed Shrimp with Champagne Vinaigrette
Veal in Rice Paper

Truffle
Broccoli Mousse with Truffle Vinaigrette
Duck Bricks

FLAVORED OILS

Bell Pepper	Halibut with Truffle and Yellow Bell Pepper Oil
	"Spiked" Sweetbreads with Red Bell Pepper Oil
	Tuna Tartare with Assorted Oils and Chips
Beet-Ginger	Sautéed Calves' Liver with Beet-Ginger Oil
Carrot-Cinnamon	Soft-Shell Crabs with Carrot-Cinnamon Oil
Chive	Millefeuille of Roquefort and Boursin
	Tuna Tartaré with Assorted Oils and Chips
	Tuna Tartare with Gaufrette Potatoes
Cinnamon	Tempura with Cabbage Salad and Cinnamon Oil
Cranberry-Orange	Venison with Cranberry-Orange Oil
Curry	Shrimp Salad with Curry Oil
	Tuna Tartare with Assorted Oils and Chips
Dill	Cold Cucumber Soup with Dill Oil
Fennel	Marinated Lemon Chicken with Fennel Oil
Ginger	Beet-Ginger Oil
Horseradish	Cod in a Horseradish Crust
	Shrimp Skewers with Oysters and Horseradish Oil
Lobster	Grilled Veal with Lobster Béarnaise
	Lobster with Parsnip Purée
	Lobster Strudel
	Shrimp, Tomato, and Cilantro Tart
	Terrine of Pasta and Crabmeat
Mustard	Rabbit Sausage with Mustard Oil
Peanut	Whiting with Endive Broth
Rosemary	Goat Cheese Bricks with Endive Salad
	Salmon Leaves with Rosemary Oil
Saffron	Sea Scallops with Garlic and Saffron Oil
Shrimp	Grilled Veal with Lobster Béarnaise
	Lobster with Parsnip Purée
	Lobster Strudel
	Shrimp, Tomato, and Cilantro Tart
	Terrine of Pasta and Crabmeat

Tomato	Red Snapper in Potato Flakes with Tomato Oil
	Sea Scallops with Garlic and Saffron Oil
Truffle	Halibut with Truffle and Yellow Bell Pepper Oil
Watercress	Goat Cheese with Watercress Oil

BROTHS

Artichoke	Lamb with Artichokes and Olives
	Scallops with Artichoke Broth
Endive	Whiting with Endive Broth
Mixed Vegetable	Black Bass in Zucchini Blossoms
	Buckwheat Pasta with Black Bass and Caviar
	Cannelloni of Crab with Cardamom
	Cold Sea Urchin Soufflé
	Crisps of Risotto
	Lobster à la Nage
	Thai Chicken Soup with Coconut Milk
Mushroom Broth	Foie Gras with Fried Leeks
	Marble of Foie Gras
	Soufflé of Foie Gras
Mushroom Syrup	Breast of Pheasant Parmentier
	Lamb in a Potato Crust
	Lamb with Wild Mushrooms
	Lobster with Parsnip Purée
	Monkfish with Mushroom Syrup
	Salmon in a Shiitake Shell
	Sautéed Foie Gras and Potato Terrine
	Squab and Lentil Salad
	Squab Purse
	Truffled Lamb with Fava Bean Purée
Shallot	Shallot Broth with Flounder
Vegetable	Beef on a String with Basil Vinaigrette
Watercress	Watercress Broth with Yellow Rice

About the Author

AT THE AGE OF SIXTEEN, JEAN-GEORGES BEGAN TRAINING IN HIS NATIVE ALSACE, IN THE KITCHENS OF L'AUBERGE DE I'LLL. THE GREAT RESTAURANT OF PAUL AND JEAN-PIERRE HAEBERLIN IS VIRTUALLY A shrine for Alsatians and all of France. Four years at Paul's side taught Jean-Georges the fundamentals of classic French cuisine, and from even the earliest days of his apprenticeship, Jean-Georges realized how fortunate he was to learn from true masters of French cuisine.

His good fortune continued in the years that followed. Jean-Georges worked with extraordinary talents: the legendary Paul Bocuse, the innovative Eckart Witzigmann in Munich, and finally Louis Outhier of L'Oasis in La Napoule-Plage on the French Riviera. Outhier sent Jean-Georges to Europe, America, and East Asia as the leader of his "flying squadron of chefs," to learn from a world of ingredients and techniques. Much of what delighted him abroad has become part of his cuisine today, and Jean-Georges says of Louis Outhier, "It was he who encouraged me to trust my instincts."

In 1984, Outhier installed Jean-Georges as chef of his newly created Marquis in Boston, which was quickly recognized as one of the leading restaurants. Then, in 1985, Louis Outhier asked Jean-Georges to join him as chef in his most ambitious project: Restaurant Lafayette in New York City.

Jean-Georges quickly learned that the tastes and desires of an American clientele were not the same as in France; New Yorkers seemed to be in more of a hurry, unaccustomed to lingering two and a half or three hours over lunch, and at times it seemed they rushed through dinner. Beyond this, he noticed they were mindful of their health and concerned about the calories of classic French cuisine.

One morning in 1987, while making himself a glass of carrot juice, Jean-Georges was inspired to try the fresh vegetable juice as a sauce for shellfish. He warmed the carrot juice, seasoned it with a pat of sweet butter and cayenne pepper, and served it as a substitute for a traditional sauce with large, lightly steamed shrimp. It was absolutely delicious. From then on he was determined to approach cooking from an entirely different direction.

Over the next thee years, Jean-Georges's cooking moved further away from classic French cuisine. Jean-Georges soon earned *The New York Times'* highest rating of four stars for his menus at Lafayette that faithfully reflected his new approach explained in this book—various dishes separated under four simple "basics" of cooking: Juices, Flavored Oils, Vinaigrettes, and Broths.

Jean-Georges, considered to be among the leading, most innovative chefs in the United States, has opened three of his own restaurants, Vong, JoJo's, and Jean Georges, all of which are among the most critically acclaimed restaurants in New York City. He creates new recipes endlessly. It was with regret that we were obliged to turn some away, marvelous as they were, so that this book could at last go to print. Those who have enjoyed the pleasure of eating at Jean-Georges's table know that his thoughts on food never stand still for long. Happily, today we can take some of his ideas and simple techniques home with us and enjoy them on our own with family and friends.

Index